*Pathways to*
*Nonprofit Excellence*

**CENTER for PUBLIC SERVICE**

The Brookings Institution established the Center for Public Service in 1999 to improve the odds that America's most talented citizens will choose careers in the public service. Toward that goal, the center is committed to rigorous research and practical recommendations for making public service more attractive, be it in traditional government settings, nonprofit agencies, or the growing number of private firms that provide services once delivered inside government. As the center's logo suggests, the single-sectored, government-centered public service of the 1970s has been replaced by a multisectored, highly mobile public service of today. The center was created to track the rise of this new public service, while making sure that both government and the nonprofit sector can compete for their fair share of talent in an ever-tightening labor market.

As part of this effort, the Center for Public Service is committed to publishing timely reports on the state of the public service. These reports, which vary in length from short reports to books, attempt to lay the foundation for long-needed policy reforms. Because these reports are designed to move quickly into publication, some will not be verified to the same level of detail as other Brookings publications. As with all Brookings publications, the judgments, conclusions, and recommendations presented in any individual study are solely those of the author or authors and should not be attributed to the trustees, officers, or other staff members of the institution.

PAUL C. LIGHT

# Pathways to
# Nonprofit Excellence

WITHDRAWN

BROOKINGS INSTITUTION PRESS
*Washington, D.C.*

Copyright © 2002
THE BROOKINGS INSTITUTION
1775 Massachusetts Avenue, N.W., Washington, D.C. 20036
www.brookings.edu

Library of Congress Cataloging-in-Publication data
Light, Paul Charles.
Pathways to nonprofit excellence / Paul C. Light.
  p.     cm.
Includes bibliographical references and index.
  ISBN 0-8157-0625-1
  1. Nonprofit organizations—Management. 2. Organizational effectiveness. 3. Leadership. I. Title.
  HD62.6 .L543 2002
  658'.048—dc21                                              2002001313

9 8 7 6 5 4 3 2 1

The paper used in this publication meets minimum requirements of the American National Standard for Information Sciences—Permanence of Paper for Printed Library Materials: ANSI Z39.48-1992.

Typeset in Sabon

Composition by R. Lynn Rivenbark
Macon, Georgia

Printed by R. R. Donnelley and Sons
Harrisonburg, Virginia

# Foreword

This is the second major report of the Nonprofit Effectiveness Project, an endeavor of the Brookings Institution's Center for Public Service. The first report, *Making Nonprofits Work*, published in 2000 and written by Paul C. Light, Douglas Dillon Senior Fellow, offered a sobering diagnosis of the state of nonprofit management reform and noted that the problem in the nonprofit sector was not too little reform, but too much. Lacking basic research on the characteristics of successful nonprofits, the sector has been deluged by wave after wave of reform over the past two decades, none of which had much chance of actually improving performance.

This second report, also written by Light, offers a more hopeful conclusion. Built on back-to-back surveys of 250 opinion leaders in the nonprofit effectiveness movement and executives at 250 high performing nonprofits those opinion leaders nominated, *Pathways to Nonprofit Excellence* offers substantive advice on both the characteristics of a well-tuned organization and where to begin the journey to improvement.

In conducting the research for this report, the Nonprofit Effectiveness Project followed many of the lessons outlined here. In its external relationships, the project made every effort to collaborate with other organizations engaged in the nonprofit effectiveness movement, including Grantmakers for Effective Organizations, the Association for Research on Nonprofit Organizations and Voluntary Action, and the Alliance for Nonprofit Management.

Light also made every effort to inform the nonprofit sector about his work. In the last year alone, he has addressed nonprofit and philanthropic groups, including the Alliance for Nonprofit Management, the Maryland Association of Nonprofit Organizations, the Ohio Association of Nonprofit Organizations, the Minnesota Council of Nonprofits, the California Association of Nonprofits, and the Donors Forum of Chicago. He also conducted site visits in Chicago, Minneapolis, and San Francisco and was guest editor of the summer 2001 edition of *The Nonprofit Quarterly*, which dealt with what it means to be nonprofit-like in a business-like world.

In addition, the project itself has involved a diverse group of funders, including the Atlantic Philanthropies, the David and Lucile Packard Foundation, the Eugene and Agnes E. Meyer Foundation, the Ewing Marion Kauffman Foundation, the Fieldstone Foundation, Grantmakers for Effective Organizations, the Irene E. and George A. Davis Foundation, and the James Irvine Foundation. In turn, these grants were administered by two institutions, Georgetown University's Public Policy Institute and the Brookings Institution, and involved a variety of research partners, including Princeton Survey Research Associates. It is hard to imagine how the project could have been more connected to the outside world.

In its internal structure, the project was built around a team of talented researchers who included project director Light, the deputy director, Judith Labiner, Princeton Survey Research Associates' Mary McIntosh, consultants Lisa Zellmer and Elizabeth Hubbard, and research assistants William Fanaras and Michael Wiesenfelder. It also benefited from the insights of seasoned advisers, including Martha Campbell at the James Irvine Foundation, Joel Fleishman at the Atlantic Philanthropies, MaryAnn Holohean at the Eugene and Agnes E. Meyer Foundation, Barbara Kibbe at the David and Lucile Packard Foundation, Robert Klitgaard, dean of the RAND Graduate School, Janine Lee at the Ewing Marion Kauffman Foundation, Ruth McCambridge at *The Nonprofit Quarterly*, and Roni Posner at the Alliance for Nonprofit Management.

In its leadership, the project benefited from Light's determination to meet the deadlines of the endeavor. Because the surveys were not completed until late fall, and the analysis not finished until Thanksgiving, Light spent December writing the report and early January making final edits to ensure that the report contained the latest insights on the impact of September 11 on the nonprofit sector. During the life of this research project, Light also completed work on another Center for Public Service report on the federal government's greatest achievements of the past fifty years, as well as a major report on the state of the federal public service.

Light could not have done this work without help from his research team, as well as his Center for Public Service team, which includes Carole Plowfield and Sherra Merchant, and the Governmental Studies program staff, which includes Susan Stewart, Elizabeth McAlpine, Gary Harding, and Gina Russo. Nor could he have succeeded without the patience of his colleagues in the Governmental Studies program, who tolerated his distraction throughout much of the past year.

Finally, the project benefited from strong management at the Brookings Institution Press. Under the guidance of Janet Walker and with editing by Venka Macintyre, proofreading by Inge Lockwood, and indexing by Scott Smiley, the report was produced in record time. Rebecca Clark, marketing director, also shaped the book with her endless enthusiasm for the project.

All in all, this report confirms that high performance among nonprofit organizations is achievable. It requires a collaborative spirit, strong teamwork, high productivity, and a commitment to results, all of which were evident here.

MICHAEL H. ARMACOST
*President*

*February 2002*
*Washington, D.C.*

# Contents

*Pathways to*
*Nonprofit Excellence*

## CHAPTER ONE

# The Nonprofit Present

The central challenge facing the nonprofit sector today is achieving and sustaining higher performance. Under increasing competition from private firms and faith-based organizations, and under duress for the disbursement crisis following the New York City and Washington tragedies, the sector's 1.23 million organizations and 11 million employees must answer the call for improvement.[1] No amount of government funding, philanthropic largesse, or program innovation will matter if the sector does not make the investments needed to both achieve and sustain high performance. The key issue today is not *what* the sector delivers, but *how* it operates.

There is no lack of reform ideas, however. The sector was awash in management reform well before the tragic events of September 11, 2001, and remains so today. Hardly a month goes by without some new suggestions for improvement, whether in the area of management standards, mergers and strategic alliances, greater transparency, or measuring outcomes. There is a reform idea for those who believe the sector is too fat and those who believe it is too lean, for those who believe it is too insular and those who believe it is becoming too much like government and the private sector, and for those who believe it is overregulated and those who believe it is underwatched.

Some of those reforms must have worked, at least according to the 500 experts interviewed for this report. Thirty percent of the respondents strongly agreed that most nonprofits are better managed today than they were five years ago, 48 percent somewhat agreed, and just 10 percent strongly or somewhat disagreed. The problem is that no one knows which reforms worked, when, and why. The sector has been so busy adopting the reform of the day that it has underinvested in basic research to measure the impact of the reforms themselves. As a result, nonprofit executives can speak a variety of reform languages but receive little help with when to use one language or another for actually improving performance. It is little wonder that reforms come and go like waves at the seashore, rarely leaving a lasting imprint on the overall performance of the sector.

The question, then, is how nonprofits can attain the organizational effectiveness needed to regain and hold the public's trust in the wake of September 11. The answer to this question lies in the lessons nonprofits have already learned about achieving and sustaining high performance. The nonprofit hardly needs to look over the border at what businesses and governments do well. It already has hundreds upon hundreds of success stories within its own midst. All it has to do is understand what those stories mean.

## The Impact of September 11

September 11 altered the future of the sector dramatically. It simultaneously affirmed the public's support for civic institutions such as the Red Cross and United Way and revealed the desperate need for a better understanding of organizational effectiveness. The sector has never been so visible, yet never so vulnerable to charges that it cannot be trusted to do the right thing. The four major responses to September 11—the surge in contributions, increased confidence in civic institutions, the disbursement crisis, and the demand for accountability—all focus squarely on performance.

### The Contributions Surge

Charitable giving increased markedly following September 11. By December 1, six in ten Americans had contributed a total of $1.5 billion to help victims in New York and Washington. Roughly $1 billion went to the Red Cross's Liberty Fund and the United Way's September 11 Fund, and a quarter went to the fifty funds established to help the victims. Mayor Rudy Giuliani's Twin Towers Fund reported $113 million in receipts, the New York Firefighters 9-11 Disaster Fund $90 million, the Robin Hood Relief Fund $48 million, and the Uniformed Firefighters Association Widow's and Children's Fund $29 million.

The funds came in all sizes, however. The Dean Street Heroes Fund raised roughly $300,000 in two months to help the families of the seven firefighters who died from Brooklyn's Engine Co. 219.[2] "It is safe to assume that every single fire company that lost somebody has a fund of some sort," said one expert. "The size will depend on how many people were lost, how large the company is, however connected they were to their community—and how affluent that community is."

This generosity has had both positive and negative effects on the non-profit sector. On the one hand, the September 11 funds may well have drawn off dollars that would have gone to other nonprofits. Much as Americans might want to give to both national and local charities, it is not clear that contributing is elastic, especially in an economic downturn.

September 11 hurt many smaller nonprofits, whether because they delayed annual fund-raising appeals, canceled performances, or curtailed services in anticipation of potential cutbacks. According to a survey of 413 California "safety net" nonprofits conducted in early December by a coalition of philanthropies called California Cares, contributions fell $25 million, or 5 to 10 percent, in the three months following September 11, in part because of the movement of contributions eastward, and in part because of an "anti-immigrant sentiment."[3] "A number of charities may not make it, and many more will drastically reduce their programs, just as they're needed most," said the head of the National Committee for Responsive Philanthropy, Rick Cohen. "This could be the most challenging time ever for the nonprofit sector."[4]

September 11 was not the most serious problem facing the sector in the third quarter of 2001, however. At most, the September 11 funds drew off no more than a fraction of the billions that went to charitable organizations in 2001. Rather, to paraphrase Bill Clinton's famous 1992 campaign slogan, the biggest problem was the economy, stupid. Not only did the recession reduce the ability of Americans to contribute, it also reduced state and local government revenues, which, in turn, reduced grants and contracts for nonprofits.

The recession also reduced peak giving among the nation's wealthiest givers. According to the *Chronicle of Philanthropy's* annual inventory of the ten largest charitable gifts, the top-ten gifts in 2001 totaled $4.6 billion, down 60 percent from the $11.1 billion in 2000.[5] Whereas the 2001 top-ten list included five high-tech givers, the 2002 list included only three. Of the three, two gave substantially less in 2001 than they had the year before. Microsoft chairman Bill Gates gave $2 billion to his Bill &

Melinda Gates Foundation in 2001, down from $5 billion in 2000, while Intel co-founder Gordon Moore gave $300 million to the California Institute of Technology in 2001, down from $5 billion the year before. "If you don't have the money," said Stacy Palmer, editor of the *Chronicle of Philanthropy*, "you can't give it away."[6]

The recession affected more than the technology giants, however. According to an October 2001 survey by the Independent Sector, three-quarters of individual donors said they would reduce or even eliminate their giving if the recession continued. In Minnesota, for example, non-profits were warned in late November to expect a 5 percent reduction in total United Way giving, while other nonprofits reported declines in their end-of-year giving campaigns that generate so much of their discretionary income every year. In New York, the 2002 state budget took what one observer calls "the worst hit to the state budget since the Great Depression. Nonprofits that rely on state money or provide services on behalf of the state are very vulnerable. We're anticipating that the non-profit work force in New York state might be reduced by 10 or 15 percent in the next year."[7]

Whether the giving glass is half full or empty depends on the ability of other, less vulnerable donors to increase their contributions to compensate for these and other shortfalls. At least according to the University of Indiana's Center on Philanthropy, the prognosis among a sample of 286 development executives and fund-raising consultants was down sharply by December. Lingering concerns about the September 11 funds and economic worries drove the center's benchmark philanthropic giving index from 91.1 on a 100-point scale in June 2001 to 83.6 in December. Unlike the Conference Board's more familiar consumer confidence index, which actually rose eight percentage points from November to December after three straight months of decline, the philanthropic giving index reached its all-time low at the same point in time. The center's present situation index, which measures the current climate for fund-raising, also hit an all-time low of 79.0, down from 89.9 in June.[8]

Despite these negative factors, the nonprofit sector may yet benefit from what some experts believe will be a surge in 2002 contributions. According to another study by the University of Indiana's Center on Philanthropy, giving has generally risen in the year following national crises such as Pearl Harbor, the Cuban missile stand-off, the Kennedy assassination, the resignation of President Richard Nixon, the 1987 financial panic, the Gulf War, the 1993 World Trade Center bombings, and the

1995 Oklahoma City bombing. Although the stock market fell in the month immediately following each of the thirteen crises studied, it rebounded the next year in all but four cases, and charitable giving grew at a greater rate in the year following each crisis in all but three cases.[9]

True to projections, the stock market had already returned to pre–September 11 levels by January 2002, raising hopes that charitable giving would not be far behind. Indeed, according to the Center on Philanthropy's analysis of its own philanthropic giving index, the best available evidence suggests "what intuition and anecdotal evidence indicate: that it has become more difficult to raise money, but that these difficulties are expected to be fairly short-lived."[10]

Reaction to the United Way scandal of the early 1990s, following its president's misuse of agency funds, suggests that current controversies surrounding it and the Red Cross will have little effect on the nonprofit sector as a whole. Although donations to the United Way did fall in the wake of the scandal, the agency's own surveys suggested that the 1991–92 economic recession was to blame.[11] Indeed, contributions to the sector actually rose 6.4 percent in 1992.

## The Confidence Curve

September 11 also produced a dramatic surge in trust in government and other civic institutions. Between July and October, the number of Americans who said they trusted the federal government to do the right thing just about always or most of the time surged from just 29 percent to 57 percent and remained perched at that level well into December. According to pre– and post–September 11 surveys conducted on behalf of the Center for Public Service, many institutions gained public confidence in the wake of the New York City and Washington attacks, including both the news media and business corporations.

No institution moved as far in this regard as the federal government, largely because it had so far to go. The number of Americans who said they trusted Washington a great deal or a fair amount jumped seventeen percentage points from July to October, while the number who felt somewhat or very favorable toward it rose twenty-eight points.[12]

Unfortunately, there is no information showing a parallel surge in trust toward the nonprofit sector immediately after September 11. Americans were asked about their confidence in just about every institution *but* the charitable organizations, which in itself is one indicator of the lack of investment in sector reform. By the time the Center for Public

Service was able to field a survey of attitudes toward the sector in December, any short-term surge had already worn down, as it had for government institutions.

There is no doubt, however, that September 11 boosted confidence in other institutions, as well as the public's trust in fellow citizens. According to a University of Chicago National Opinion Research Center (NORC) survey of more than 2,100 Americans taken in the two weeks following the tragedies, almost half of the respondents made contributions to charities in this period, and a quarter donated or tried to donate blood. The vast majority also said "special prayers," while substantial percentages reported greater faith in their fellow citizens. Two-thirds said that most people are helpful, up twenty-one percentage points from 1996 NORC surveys, while three-fifths said most people in general are fair, up 12 percent.[13] "Bowling Alone" Harvard scholar Robert Putnam found similar results in his own post–September 11 survey: "Whites trust blacks more, Asians trust Latinos more, and so on, than these very same people did a year ago," he wrote. "Evidence of enhanced trust across ethnic and other social divisions is especially striking and gratifying."[14]

This general rise in social trust tracks a broad increasee in all forms of civic engagement following September 11. By the weekend of October 5–8, when a Wirthlin Worldwide survey of 1,009 Americans was conducted, 58 percent of Americans had made a charitable contribution, up nine percentage points from the NORC survey completed two weeks earlier. All totaled, seven out of ten Americans gave money, time, or blood in direct response to September 11.

It is important to note that trust in charitable organizations was already remarkably high before September 11, thereby limiting the potential surge associated with the tragedies. According to a July 2001 survey conducted on behalf of the Independent Sector, 90 percent of Americans said they had a lot or some confidence in the nation's charitable organizations, and 85 percent said the same of federated appeals such as the United Way and March of Dimes. Unlike confidence in the federal government, in President George W. Bush, Vice President Dick Cheney, and presidential appointees, which had substantial room to rise after the attacks, trust in the nonprofit sector had little room to go.

Trust in the government and the nonprofit sector are not necessarily linked, however. Independent Sector surveys have shown steady confidence in the sector's ability to deliver goods and services on the public's behalf. Between 1994 and 1999, for example, Independent Sector's

*Giving and Volunteering in the United States* surveys showed relative stability in the number of Americans who believe that nonprofit organizations play a major role in their communities.

In 1994, 73 percent said charitable organizations play a major role in making our communities better places to live, compared with 71 percent in 1996 and 76 percent in 1999. Somewhat smaller majorities also said that charitable organizations are honest and ethical in their use of donated funds, play an important role in speaking out on important issues, and are more effective in providing services than they were five years ago.[15] Although there are some troubling signs in the data, including a slight decline in the number of Americans who said the need for charitable organizations is greater now than five years ago (down from 82 percent in 1994 to 74 percent in 1999), most of the trend lines are in the right direction and show little of the characteristic distrust that Americans feel toward government.

Nevertheless, a January 2002 survey by ABC News suggests that the surge in confidence is restricted almost entirely to the war on terrorism. Whereas 68 percent of Americans trusted the federal government almost always or most of the time on matters concerning national security, only 38 percent felt the same about the federal government on social issues such as the economy, health care, Social Security, and education.[16]

### The Disbursement Crisis

September 11 also cast an ominous shadow over the nonprofit sector, raising questions about the ability of its flagship organizations to spend money wisely. Like the United Way scandal of the early 1990s, September 11 may yet be remembered by nonprofits more for the scathing scrutiny it has produced than for the resulting surge in confidence in government and its civic partners.

Much of the scrutiny was driven by Bill O'Reilly, the pugnacious anchor of Fox News Channel's *The O'Reilly Factor.* O'Reilly was the first to exploit the sluggish disbursement of the Red Cross Liberty Fund, the largest of the September 11 funds. The Red Cross was guilty not just of bureaucratic sloth, O'Reilly charged, but of diverting at least some of the Liberty Fund to administrative needs.

In a sense, the Red Cross became a victim of the public's generosity because the outpouring revealed the weaknesses in the organization's infrastructure. It did not have the refrigerators to store all the blood that had been donated and desperately needed new telecommunications and information systems to distribute the money quickly and wisely. In addition, internal policies designed to protect the privacy of beneficiaries prohibited the Red Cross from participating in developing a master list of victims that could be shared by the hundreds of other relief agencies engaged in the legitimate effort to help the families of the 3,000 victims of the disaster.

Unlike many private corporations, which would have moved quickly to address the charges, the Red Cross decided to stand behind legalese. Led by its fiery president, former U.S. surgeon general Bernadine Healy, the Red Cross noted that all of its calls for donations had contained fine print clearly stating that the Liberty Fund was to be used "for this tragedy and emerging needs from this event." "Together we can save a life," each of the public service advertisements ended.

O'Reilly countered that the fine print was irrelevant given the banner headlines promising that contributions would be used to "help save lives." Although O'Reilly and others argued that the advertisements created an implied compact between donors and the Red Cross, Healy did not believe she was creating that expectation:

> She didn't call it the Sept. 11 Fund, after all. And Healy said she felt that the Red Cross needed to plan ahead at the same time as it dealt with the crisis of the moment creatively. So while she set up a cash gift program for victims' families, which was novel for the Red Cross, she also seized the opportunity to beef up some expensive pet projects that had gained new urgency—the weapons-of-mass-destruction-preparedness program and the creation of a strategic reserve of frozen blood. She thought this was logical, but she didn't initially bother to explain herself to the American public.[17]

The controversy seemed tailor-made for *The O'Reilly Factor*, which features a point-counterpoint format on issues of the day. On October 5, for example, the program featured Healy and New York State Attorney General Eliot Spitzer. Starting his nightly "Unresolved Problem" segment with Lynda Fiori, a young widow with two children who had lost her husband in the World Trade Center collapse, O'Reilly then moved to the following exchange with Spitzer:

O'REILLY: Ms. Fiori was assured that she would be helped by this agency. They've raised more—you know, millions of dollars for their foundation. She hasn't gotten anything from them. Are you going to look into that?

SPITZER: Well, what we are looking into, Bill, and I think you're highlighting in a specific case a very overarching problem, we want to make sure that the hundreds of millions of dollars, nearly a billion dollars, as you say, that has been given so generously by the American public ends up where it should go, that the people who need the help get that help, and we will be working with the charities to make sure that they understand where people need assistance, they don't duplicate, they don't waste the money. That is what our objective here has been.

O'REILLY: So you're the guy then. You're in charge. You're the point man. You're going to make sure it happens and that this money isn't stolen.

SPITZER: We are—we are going to make sure that it isn't stolen, we are going to try to provide guidance to people in the form of information and we—we think there's a public trust here, and we think that the public trust is going to be protected.

O'REILLY: Well, it has to be. If it isn't . . . .

SPITZER: Absolutely.

O'REILLY: . . . Everybody in New York State who's involved is going to be in trouble because I'm going to lay it out.[18]

Only later did O'Reilly note that the Red Cross had mailed Ms. Fiori a check soon after the attacks.

The Red Cross was not the only target of O'Reilly's anger. He also singled out the many celebrities who had donated their time for the fund-raising telethons that followed September 11. As O'Reilly told the *New York Post* in early November, "They get a lot of publicity when they do these events, but when it's time to take some responsibility, they are MIA. . . . We are still talking with some celebrities, and will hope a few of them will step up, but the majority of these people are phonies, much more interested in their own images than solving any social problems."[19] Eventually, James Brown, Clint Eastwood, Goldie Hawn, and Kurt Russell all appeared on O'Reilly's program, while George Clooney later released an open letter accusing O'Reilly of misleading the public in an effort to boost his program's ratings, which were soaring.

Under attack from O'Reilly and a growing number of oversight groups, Healy resigned on October 26 in an elaborate pageant designed to minimize the turmoil at her agency. Three weeks later, on November 14, the Red Cross announced that it would restrict distribution of money from the Liberty Fund to people directly affected by September 11. "The people of this country have given the Red Cross their hard-earned dollars, their trust and very clear direction for our September 11 relief efforts," said David McLaughlin, chairman of the agency's board. "Regrettably, it took us too long to hear their message. Now we must change course to restore the faith of our donors and the trust of Americans."[20]

O'Reilly took credit for Healy's resignation in a *Washington Times* op-ed piece published on November 19, declaring that the "Red Cross has surrendered," while castigating the national media for their inattention and promising further inquiry into the "charity chaos" at the United Way of America: "I have zeroed in on the 'September 11 Fund' run by the United Way and a New York bank," he wrote. "That's the fund that received all the money from the TV telethon and the big New York concert. We're talking $337 million here. And there is no question that the United Way is having trouble getting those funds directly to the grieving families. The reason is the United Way contracts out to local charities to actually hand the money to the families. And some of those charities are inefficient, to say the least. The entire situation is a big mess."[21]

Where ratings lead, Congress is almost sure to follow, which it did with a hearing before the House Committee on Energy and Commerce on November 6. The hearing generated more heat than light as one committee member after another attacked the Red Cross and its now former president, Healy. "Something's wrong," said chairman Billy Tauzin (R-Louisiana), promising future oversight hearings on the state of the nonprofit sector. "I think you took advantage of a very tragic situation," said Representative Bart Stupak (D-Michigan), accusing the Red Cross of using money from the Liberty Fund to cross-subsidize its long-term institutional needs.[22] Whatever else can be said about the need to invest in organizational infrastructure *before* a crisis, the problems surrounding nonprofit performance and stewardship did not leave Washington, D.C., with Bernadine Healy.

As if to make the case, O'Reilly turned to the United Way as his next target in a November 26, 2001, exchange with September 11 Fund director and former U.S. comptroller Joshua Gotbaum. O'Reilly started by listing some of the organizations that had already received grants, including the Brooklyn Philharmonic, the Jennifer Muller Dance Troupe, a digital art studio called Three-Legged Dog, the Arab American Support

Center, and the Asian American Legal Defense and Education Fund. He then launched into a scathing attack on administrative excess:

> The fact is that the United Way has changed the mandate in mid-stream, saying now that the entire September 11 Fund will not go directly to the grieving families, as was the telethon pitch. In the new turn, the fund will go toward, quote, "immediate and longer-term needs of the victims, their families, and communities affected by the tragedy." So now the canvas is much wider, and some Americans believe they've been snookered. So the right thing is for the United Way to give refunds if people want them. A canceled check or credit card slip would be proof. If it is not willing to do that, it will be forever marked as an outfit that cannot be trusted.

O'Reilly moved through the interview with typical speed and increasing vitriol, eventually trapping Gotbaum on a simple point: the September 11 Fund would not take any administrative fees from its $343 million but would allow grantees to charge administrative overhead.

> O'REILLY: All right, now, look, you're dancing, and I'm getting steamed. You say you're not taking any administrative costs, and I believe you.
> GOTBAUM: That's right.
> O'REILLY: But that's a shell game, if you're giving to other people who are taking administrative costs out.
> GOTBAUM: Bill, I got to tell you, I don't agree with you, and here's why. . . . It is a fact that we fund the cost of delivering services to the victims and their families. And the reason we do that is because if we said "We don't pay for the rent to deliver this, or for the . . . payrolls of the people who do it," if we waited until we had volunteer people and volunteer facilities and volunteer computers, the victims would be waiting until Kingdom come. . . .
> O'REILLY: All right, but listen, Mr. Gotbaum, you're pettifogging this issue like crazy. But you're doing a dance, and I don't think you should be doing that.[23]

Disbursement is not the only issue surrounding the collection of disaster funds. Victims are sharply divided on the most basic questions of need as relief agencies attempt to value the lives of the firefighters and police officers versus bond traders, receptionists, and bystanders. "The Declaration of Independence says all men are created equal," William Doyle, a spokesman for Give Your Voice, a newly created organization for the families of New York's civilian victims, later told the *Washington Post*. "There is no way there is equality in this situation."[24]

The divisions will almost certainly grow as an open-ended federal compensation fund begins disbursing aid. Overseen by a special master picked by the Department of Justice, the fund could eventually grow to $11 billion and covers those killed or injured in the attacks or in its "immediate aftermath." The fund, which was created by Congress almost immediately after the attacks, leaves a number of questions unanswered, including the definition of what constitutes an injury.

Because each award will be based in part on estimated lifetime earnings, the formula will produce wildly different awards. When coupled with the private insurance and pension holdings that some victims held, the eventual sorting out may well produce a sense of winners and losers based on class, race, and gender, which in turn is likely to ignite further debate about fairness and stewardship. "This money should really go where it's needed," the widow of the owner of a concierge service who was killed in the World Trade Center collapse told the *Post*. "Obviously, if you have a home and you have two cars—you have a Mercedes and a Lexus—you're in a lot better shape than somebody who doesn't own anything—a home or a car—and has a bunch of kids and has no way to make a living. . . . There needs to be some way to decide whose needs are greater."[25]

### The Demand for Accountability

Even if O'Reilly were to suddenly turn away from the story, the nonprofit sector can expect intense scrutiny far into the future. Oversight groups have moved quickly to link the Red Cross and United Way controversies to their long-standing calls for greater accountability, while the mainstream media have been on the issue for several months now.

On the oversight front, the Better Business Bureau's Wise Giving Alliance alerted the press to the accountability issue on October 17, 2001, when it re-released a spring 2001 public opinion survey under a new headline, "Donors Expect Charities to Adhere to Ethical Standards." The link to September 11 was obvious:

"Donors most definitely want to hold charities accountable for their use of funds, but the inability to access information often stands in their way," said Art Taylor, president and CEO of the BBB Wise Giving Alliance (the Alliance), the organization that sponsored the survey. "Most people (70%) say it is difficult to tell whether a charity soliciting their contribution is legitimate, and many (72%) also say it is difficult to choose between organizations that raise money for similar causes."

These difficulties were dramatically highlighted in the past month as Americans attempted to respond to the needs of those impacted by the September 11 terrorist attacks. A high volume of inquiries to the Alliance substantiated the eagerness of donors to give, and gave voice to widespread questions about how to evaluate the accuracy of the charity appeals/promotions and the effectiveness of the many disaster relief programs.

Just to make sure the point was not lost on a news-weary public, the Wise Giving Alliance re-re-released the survey on November 1, this time under the headline "Accountability Challenge for Charities," with a much more explicit lead:

> The acts of September 11 touched all Americans in an unprecedented way and continue to present new and unexpected challenges. Yet, one of the most remarkable consequences of these events was not in itself surprising—the outpouring of contributions to help victims of the disaster. Overwhelmingly, Americans stepped up to the plate, giving freely and in good faith. Knowledgeable estimates place the gifts at one billion dollars and growing. Now, the challenge rests squarely with the charitable sector to be equally forthcoming regarding the use of these donations.
>
> The stakes are high. How recipient organizations spend these funds, their success in addressing both immediate and longer term needs, and perhaps most of all, their willingness to make prompt public disclosure of their activities, will strongly impact future charitable giving. Donors want to support charities but this desire is coupled with high expectations for charity accountability.

The Wise Giving Alliance was not the only oversight group to link its work on accountability to September 11. The American Institute of Philanthropy, which has been called "the pitbull of watchdogs," issued a "special alert" titled "Disaster Strikes America" in October that featured a color picture of the World Trade Center collapse: "Tragedy has struck our nation's capital and financial nerve center. After the September 11, 2001 disaster it is natural to want to help the victims of this crisis. Let your anguish and pain motivate you to help but please use your head to make an informed and thoughtful giving decision. Anytime there is a highly publicized crisis there are plenty of scammers coming out of the woodwork that will be more than happy to take advantage of your good intentions and help you to squander your charitable dollars."

Nor was Fox News the only media outlet to focus on the disbursement controversy. By December, the story had moved from heavy daily coverage to mainstream monthly magazines such as *Money*, which urged its nearly 2 million readers to use its "Wise Giving Guide" to avoid the disbursement "logjam": "For donors, this logjam, though likely to be resolved soon, offers important lessons on the best way to give. In the days following September 11, all that was called for was generosity. Now, as we try to return to our more normal patterns and contemplate year-end giving, what's needed is a more deliberate approach to charitable giving."[26]

The "Wise Giving Guide" featured eight recommendations that seemed designed to raise donor distrust toward the very organizations they wanted to support:

1. Establish your goals and budget.
2. Be sure that the group is a charity.
3. Know what work your dollars will support.
4. Examine the finances.
5. Understand what the numbers won't tell you.
6. Check with the watchdogs.
7. Consider what can cut into your donation.
8. Stay involved.

There is nothing wrong with the advice per se, but the tone is clearly cautionary. *Money* recommends, for example, that donors weigh a charity's financial stability by checking for asset reserves (part 1, line 21 of the Internal Revenue Service Form 990): "Maintaining one to three years' worth of revenues (line 12) is health," writes *Money*, "but more may be a sign that the group is stockpiling money rather than spending it on programs."

*Money* also rightly warns that financial ratios have limitations, but only to reinforce the point that nonprofits sometimes lie. "Nonprofit accounting rules give charities considerable latitude in how they allocate expenses among program services, management and fundraising," *Money* writes in quoting an expert on Form 990. "Try to dig beyond the numbers by talking to people in the community who work with the charity— what does the neurologist next door think of your local MS chapter—as well as those the group aids."

Even *Money's* advice to stay involved is tinged with distrust: "With a local group, your time and efforts can often have a big impact. Be sure to keep monitoring your charities to make sure they live up to their promises. If they consistently fall short of their goals, it may be best to shift your giving elsewhere—right now, especially, there's no shortage of good causes." *Money* advances that search by listing seven lesser-known charities that "keep overhead costs in check," including America's Second Harvest (with 14–23 percent fund-raising costs and a B+ American Institute of Philanthropy mission rating), Boys and Girls Clubs of America (9 percent costs, A rating), Elizabeth Glaser Pediatric Aids Foundation (8 percent costs, A+ rating), the International Rescue Committee (8 percent costs, A+ rating), National Mental Health Association (7 percent costs, A+ rating), Reading Is Fundamental (13 percent costs, A rating), and Trust for Public Land (13 percent costs, A rating).

## The Uncertainty Factor

Together, the affirmations, disappointments, and demand for greater accountability create significant uncertainties for the future of the nonprofit sector. According to a November 2001 study by CompassPoint, the majority of nonprofits in the San Francisco area believe that 2002 will be a difficult year, although few see themselves immediately at risk. Nonprofits were already hedging their bets by scaling back expenses, increasing fund-raising calls, and freezing pay and hiring, even as they grappled with increased demand due to the economic slowdown.[27]

There is also some evidence that the Red Cross and United Way controversies may yet take their toll on trust in the sector. According to a Center for Public Service survey conducted in mid-December 2001, 60 percent of Americans said they were following the Red Cross/United Way story very or fairly closely.[28] It ranked number five on the public's news agenda in mid-December, ahead of the death of former Beatle George Harrison and the Enron bankruptcy: (1) terrorist attacks on the United States (89 percent of the public said it was following the story very or fairly closely); (2) the military effort in Afghanistan (84 percent);

(3) reports about the condition of the U.S. economy (77 percent); (4) continued violence in the Middle East (71 percent); (5) the controversy over how the Red Cross and United Way plan to use the funds given to help victims of the September 11 tragedies (60 percent); (6) the bankruptcy of Enron Corporation (34 percent); (7) the death of former Beatle George Harrison (33 percent).

At least in the aggregate, confidence in the sector remained high despite this attention. Asked how much confidence they had in charitable organizations, 86 percent of Americans answered that they had "a lot" or "some" confidence in charitable organizations in the December Center for Public Service survey, compared with 91 percent in a July Independent Sector survey. Similarly, when asked how much confidence they had in federated appeals such as the United Way and the March of Dimes, 83 percent of Americans said they had "a lot" or "some" confidence in December, compared with 85 percent in July.[29]

Aggregate numbers do not tell the whole story, however. As table 1-1 shows, although the number of Americans who said they had a lot of confidence in charitable organizations remained unchanged in the July and December surveys, the number who had a lot of confidence in federated appeals fell by more than a third. Whereas 39 percent of Americans had a lot of confidence in federated appeals in July, only 26 percent felt the same way in December.

Because the July question about charitable organizations did not include a reference to the Red Cross, it is difficult to know what effect, if any, the Red Cross controversy had on the December responses. And because the July question about federated appeals included a reference to both the United Way and March of Dimes, it is difficult to attribute all of the decline to the United Way controversy.

However, half of the December sample was asked two slightly amended versions of the July questions: (1) "How much confidence do you have in charitable organizations *such as the Red Cross?*" and (2) "How much confidence do you have in federated appeals such as the United Way?" The first question focused specifically on the Red Cross as an example of a charitable organization, while the second dropped the reference to the March of Dimes, leaving the United Way as the only example of a federated appeal.[30]

Table 1-1 shows that the December respondents had much higher confidence in charitable organizations when the question included the Red Cross as a reference point. Despite two months of controversy, the sector

Table 1-1. *Confidence in the Nonprofit Sector, 2001*[a]

Percent

| Month | Confidence in charitable organizations | | Confidence in federated appeals | |
|---|---|---|---|---|
| | Charitable organizations | Charitable organizations such as the Red Cross | Federated appeals such as United Way and March of Dimes | Federated appeals such as United Way |
| *A lot of confidence* | | | | |
| July | 25 | Not asked | 39 | Not asked |
| December | 24 | 41 | 26 | 27 |
| *Some confidence* | | | | |
| July | 65 | Not asked | 46 | Not asked |
| December | 62 | 48 | 58 | 50 |
| *None* | | | | |
| July | 8 | Not asked | 13 | Not asked |
| December | 7 | 9 | 13 | 17 |

a. N = 4,216 for Independent Sector, July 2001; 1,011 for Center for Public Service, December 2001.

still fared better with the Red Cross than without it. However, the absence of a surge in confidence toward charitable organizations before and after September 11 is telling, particularly given the extraordinary surge in other institutions. The question is not why confidence in charitable organizations remained the same, but why it did not soar. The Red Cross may well be the answer. Here, the December survey suggests that the Red Cross controversy may have acted as a brake on public confidence, freezing it at its pre-September levels as the story escalated.

Table 1-1 also shows that confidence in federated appeals remained virtually the same regardless of how the question was asked. Because respondents generally focus on the first example in any list of "such as's," the drop in confidence in federated appeals such as the United Way and the March of Dimes is best viewed as a decline in confidence mostly in the United Way. Here, the December survey suggests that the United Way controversy caused actual damage to public confidence, whether because it reminded Americans of the 1992 United Way scandal or because trust in federated appeals is softer to begin with.

Whatever the case, the data seem to confirm the link between trust and actual performance. To the extent nonprofit organizations such as the

Red Cross and United Way prove effective in combating terrorism and helping victims, they might regain the trust they either lost or did not gain in the wake of September 11. Performance, not promises, is the currency of public confidence today, which means that organizational effectiveness has never been more important.

## Conclusion

Americans knew a great deal about individual nonprofit organizations long before September 11, whether through their giving, volunteering, or own needs. But they knew less about the sector as a sum of its parts. Absent a conversation about what it means to be nonprofit in this moment of intense scrutiny, the sector risks being defined by Bill O'Reilly and others like him as an overgrown, inept, bureaucratic, duplicative, money-hungry, and insensitive segment of modern society. This is not what nonprofits are about, and it is a view that must change.

The rest of this report explains what nonprofits are really like and shows that continuous improvement and high performance can be a goal of a nonprofit organization. Chapter 2 explores competing scenarios of the future. Chapters 3 and 4 discuss the characteristics of high-performing nonprofits culled from back-to-back surveys of 250 opinion leaders in the organizational effectiveness movement and the executives of 250 organizations they admire (for the results of these surveys, see appendixes A and B). And chapter 5 examines the different pathways to higher performance in more detail.

Overall, this report shows nonprofits can achieve high performance either the hard way or the easy way. The hard way consists of needless bureaucracy, overburdened leaders, antiquated systems, and constant stress; the easy way consists of investments in structures, systems, training, and leadership, all of which will create organizations that excel more naturally. "I have seen incapable organizations that are very effective," said one of the grantmakers interviewed for this report. "I know it sounds crazy, but they are not taking capacity seriously. They do not have boards that function properly . . . not illegally, but just not optimally. But they can only go on like that for a while."

There is no one best way to achieve and sustain natural high performance, however. As the title of this report suggests, nonprofits can pursue improvement along several pathways, each one having its own strengths and weaknesses. But whatever pathway they choose, nonprofits will not achieve high performance by pretending to be something other than what they are. They are not corporations, small businesses, governments, faith-based organizations, or firms, even if they behave like all of the above from time to time. They are nonprofits and must become more nonprofit-like if they are to choose their future.

## CHAPTER TWO

# Imagining a
# Nonprofit-like Future

As the nation recovers from September 11, the nonprofit sector faces a range of possible futures. For example, the sector may emerge from recent events stronger than ever, buoyed by public recognition that it is as much a part of homeland defense as airport security. Americans may redouble their giving and volunteering as a way to express a renewed sense of civic connection. And even the government may increase giving as a way to stimulate the economy and help the needy.

Tempting though it is to plan for the best, the future is much too uncertain to assume that the nonprofit sector will rebound quickly from the recent economic decline and disbursement crisis. Three more likely futures ten years from now are a winnowing, withering, or awakening of the sector, each of which would leave it with a different size and shape.

Recent events such as the Red Cross and United Way controversies and short-term reductions in revenue may well produce a sharp reduction in the total number of nonprofits through mergers, acquisitions, alliances, and the mortality of thousands of relatively small, young organizations. This winnowing would leave the sector with fewer but bigger nonprofits, though not necessarily fewer employees, which would be much the same effect that the merger and acquisition fury of the 1980s and 1990s had on the private sector.

Recent events could also trigger a general shrinkage among individual nonprofits, but little in the way of mergers and mortality. Depending upon the length of the economic downturn and contribution flows following September 11, many nonprofits might starve themselves into a weakened organizational state. Although the withering would cause some smaller nonprofits to fold, its main effect would be to stop the creation of new nonprofits for a time, while freezing employment at current levels.

Finally, the future could produce an emphasis on higher performance across the sector. Driven by a new golden rule, whereby nonprofits would be exhorted to "do unto themselves before others do unto them," this awakening would require a heavier investment in management systems, training, and capacity building across the sector, as well as acknowledgment that nonprofits need operating support and overhead to sustain high performance over time. This awakening also involves what venture philanthropist Mario Marino calls a "tipping point" scenario in which "public and private funders collaborate with nonprofits to increase the effectiveness of the nonprofit sector. Because of increasing resource constraints, grantmakers and grantees become more strategic in their decisions. They become even more concerned about concentrating resources on the areas with the greatest potential for social impact (e.g., early-childhood education). They increase their focus on scale, consolidation, and collaboration to spread good models and minimize the all-too-common exercise of reinventing wheels."

## Choosing a Nonprofit-like Future

The nonprofit sector can always let the future take its own course by refusing to choose among the competing scenarios. But in doing so, it would almost surely experience either the withering that comes from inaction or the winnowing that comes from external criticism. It can only reap the benefits of the reengineering and awakening by deliberate choice.

The challenge is how to take hold of the future and shape it deliberately. Improving sector performance is not merely a matter of adopting the latest reform fad, be it greater transparency, tightened financial controls, more collaboration, or fixed administrative costs. Despite some evidence that nonprofit management has improved over the past five years, one can argue the sector has not improved fast enough or gone far enough to meet the increased expectations of the public described above. Moreover, merely dipping into the vast inventory of reform ideas pulsing through the sector will hardly reassure reluctant funders, impatient legislators, and oversight groups that the sector is committed to sustainable improvement.

### Rejecting Business-like

At the core of winnowing and withering is the sense that the nonprofit sector should somehow become leaner, tougher, and more efficient, in a word, more "business-like." To some extent, awakening also calls for more business-like practices as a means of achieving greater efficiency, accountability, and responsiveness. At the same time, it generally avoids the corporate rhetoric so often associated with bottom-line management.

Some nonprofits have resisted the pressure to become more business-like precisely because they have watched a host of private and government reforms of this nature fail. They rightly wonder whether total quality management in the private sector or reinventing government in the public sector made much difference. As it turns out, reform often does more harm than good. According to a 2001 summer survey by the Center for Public Service, almost half of the federal employees whose organizations had been reinvented said the changes made their jobs either somewhat or a lot more difficult to do.[1]

Others do not know which businesses to copy. Two years ago, some nonprofit boards would have applauded the executive director who said, "Our organization should be more like Cisco." After all, the company had just experienced four years of record earnings and was the largest private corporation in the world. Two years ago, some also would have applauded the director who declared, "Let's be more like Enron." The company was the fastest-growing energy trader in the world and was named the nation's most innovative company by *Fortune* for six years running.

Nevertheless, the allure of being business-like remains, in part because the private sector disposes of its failures much more efficiently than does the nonprofit sector or government. Today's *Fortune 500* of America's leading corporations contains a good number that were not in operation thirty years ago and omits those now long gone. Government agencies obviously have much higher survival rates, prompting former Brookings Institution scholar Herbert Kaufman to write a book titled *Are Governmental Organizations Immortal?*[2] Nonprofit agencies are not without their own survival strategies. Although individual organizations do die from time to time, often because of poor financial planning, their

501(c)(3) charters can live on indefinitely, searching for some new leader or idea to give them a chance to operate again.

The private sector also tolerates very high mortality rates among its new products and innovations. For every new product that succeeds, there are literally thousands that fail. This high tolerance of failure, not to mention the tax write-offs that go with it, gives the private sector an enormous advantage as a source of innovation and change. Whereas government and nonprofit organizations must struggle mightily to bring even one new idea to scale, private firms can amass huge amounts of capital solely on the basis of promised rewards. The dot.com revolution, and its collapse, stand as stark evidence of this.

## Defining Nonprofit-Like

The emphasis on being business-like is especially marked among board members, business schools, and for-profit consulting firms. In their view, the approach can be transferred smoothly across sectoral lines. Many even promise performance gains that private firms and government agencies long ago abandoned as unrealistic under the best of circumstances.

Few nonprofits would ignore promising reforms just because they come from the private sector or government, nor, for that matter, should the private sector and government ignore reforms that come from the nonprofit sector, particularly when they relate to perseverance, doing more with less, community building, or the faithful execution of a business plan or law. The private sector was hardly the first to discover the merits of flat organization charts, for example, nor was government the first to recognize the benefits of listening to communities. Both organizational reforms have long been associated with the nonprofit sector. Few nonprofits would also dismiss the need to compete, slim down, join alliances, and so forth. Most nonprofits exist in a turbulent, competitive world and must often compete not just against other nonprofits, but against governmental and private organizations alike. Name an area of nonprofit endeavor and there is likely to be some for-profit, governmental, or blended alternative, be it in the arts, environmental protection, child care, or advocacy for the poor. Witness the trisector, performance-based, welfare-to-work tournaments in San Diego County, California, and Milwaukee County, Wisconsin, where private firms (Maximus and IMS) compete head-to-head with nonprofit agencies (Catholic Charities and Goodwill Industries), nonprofit/private partnerships, and the remnants of the two county welfare bureaucracies.[3]

As they spend time together, however, organizations tend to become more alike than different. The more they share best practices, provide similar services, import ideas across sectoral boundaries, or take funds from the same sources, the more they become like each other. This "institutional isomorphism," as sociologists label it, may be the most significant concern for the faith-based organizations about to take their first federal grants from the Bush administration. At least in organizational life, familiarity breeds similarity.

Thus the question is not whether nonprofits need to become more effective and efficient, but how far they can go in being business-like without altering their character. How much money, for example, can nonprofits make through sales and fees before they become more like a business than a nonprofit? How much pressure to compete can they tolerate before the collaboration that makes them part of the community in which they reside suffers, or the pressure to be lean and mean becomes more compelling than the pressure to help the community? Much as competition can sharpen the organizational senses, it can also keep nonprofits on a "treadmill," where they spend more time searching for the next dollar or innovation than fine-tuning what they already know works in enhancing their impacts.

Unless the nonprofit sector soon finds a second, equally compelling pathway toward higher performance, it will have to find the balance between being business-like and being nonprofit-like on its own. If they stay on the business path, some nonprofits will drift toward private status, leaving gaps in the nonprofit fabric of their communities. Others will move from business fad to fad with no compass to guide their choices or will stand frozen as they try to determine how to be business-like in a nonprofit world. And others will become business/nonprofit hybrids, members of a strange new league of organizations that may yet test the federal tax laws protecting charitable organizations, soon to be joined perhaps by the faith-based organizations being drawn across the boundary between church and state. "If [nonprofits] choose to compete, they must do it whole hog," writes SURDNA Foundation president Edward Skloot. "They can distinguish themselves by systematically investing in [information technology], in management, and in their employees. By upgrading themselves, they upgrade their ability to compete and to advocate. If they do that, they will also advance their values of inclusion, civic engagement, democratic participation, and community building."[4]

## From Condition to Aspiration

One reason being business-like remains so popular is that the nonprofit sector has yet to build a distinctive, aspirational definition of the term "nonprofit-like." Whereas "business-like" conjures up images of competitive, entrepreneurial, strategic, agile, efficient, effective innovative, and profitable entities, "nonprofit-like" is associated with being a sluggish, underfunded, stressful, duplicative, inefficient, and tax-exempt, 501(c)(3) organization. "The word "nonprofit" is probably the most horrible thing we have ever done to ourselves," said one technical assistance provider interviewed for this report. "The only thing we seem to value in this country today is whether an organization makes money or not. We don't, or at least we supposedly don't. People think that is what the word means. We are defined by what we are not, and even that is not a clear definition. We are not defined by what we are."

Among the recent graduates of the nation's top public policy and administration schools, the private sector, not government or the nonprofit sector, is seen as the sector most likely to spend public money wisely, while government is seen as the best place to represent the public interest. Although the nonprofit sector has become the destination of choice for recent graduates who want to help people, it is also the sector least likely to hold graduates over time. Only 44 percent of graduates who started their careers in the nonprofit sector were still there when our survey research team interviewed them in 1999, compared with 51 percent of those who started in the private sector, and 57 percent who started in government.[5]

The first step in redeeming the concept of being nonprofit-like is to convert it from a conditional state to a goal. Like "business-like," "nonprofit-like" should not have negative overtones. Properly defined, the term should refer to the best in the sector, whatever that benchmark might be, and it should be aspirational in tone. At a minimum, it should refer to high performance in the service of the public good and not to being mediocre or hanging on for survival's sake. This meaning emphasizes dedication not only to excellence but also to the public, not private, good.

Some might argue that "nonprofit-like" should also denote advocacy on behalf of stakeholders, efforts to build community, and collaboration in pursuit of economic, social, political, or artistic renewal, or that it should include operational goals such as cost efficiency, outcomes measurement, total quality management, even customer satisfaction. Others emphasize another sense of the word as well: that of being responsive, trustworthy, or faithful. Whatever the final list of strategies, operational goals, and core values, the debate over what it means to be nonprofit-like is long overdue. Until the sector sets down its own terms of higher performance, it is likely to be shaped by fads and fashions imported from government and business and thus may become less nonprofit-like over time.

## Investing in Effectiveness

This is a particularly good moment for the nonprofit sector to make the commitment to higher performance. There are more cheerleaders, funders, and advocates of improvement than ever before, not to mention consultants, graduate schools, and researchers. The energy surrounding the general notion that nonprofits should improve has never been greater. Grantmakers for Effective Organizations, which was founded in 1998 as an affinity group of the Council of Foundations, now numbers 400 members and continues to grow at a record-setting pace. The Alliance for Nonprofit Management, which was formed to improve technical assistance to the sector in 1998, now has a membership of 625 and also continues to grow. *The Nonprofit Quarterly*, which was relaunched in 2000 as a national source of advice on building capacity, has more than quadrupled its subscription base to 4,500.

Equally important, funding for organizational effectiveness has never been higher. According to the Foundation Center, grants for capacity building—for things such as "management development," "technical assistance," and "program evaluation"—totaled $400 million in 1999, up from $300 million the year before. Although the Foundation Center did not track management development and evaluation grants until the late 1990s and does not include the capacity building embedded in the new venture philanthropy, the trends are all in the right direction. Hence technical assistance grants rose from $59 million in 1989 to $166 million in 1999, a 180 percent increase over the decade.[6]

Unfortunately, the nonprofit sector does not know enough yet about how to achieve higher performance to embrace this more hopeful future. Despite promising new case work by the Wilder Foundation, McKinsey

& Company, the Morino Institute, the Urban Institute, the Kaufman Foundation, the Mary Reynolds Babock Foundation, and InnoNet (a Washington, D.C., evaluation firm), the sector remains awash in reform fads as nonprofits and their funders search for interventions that might make a difference.

## Waves of Reform

Nonprofits are buffeted by the same waves of reform that affect private and governmental organizations. As I argued in *Making Nonprofits Work*, at least four tides, or philosophies, of reform are currently moving across the nonprofit sector: (1) scientific management, which focuses on standards of excellence; (2) liberation management, which emphasizes revising the rules that prevent program success; (3) war on waste, which stresses the sector's overbuilt and underdisciplined approach to spending; and (4) watchful eye, which centers on the need for greater disclosure and sunshine on individual nonprofits.[7]

Each reform philosophy uses different enforcement mechanisms. Scientific management relies on certification systems and celebration to forge a set of common characteristics that its advocates believe will produce higher performance; liberation management carefully measures inputs, activities, outputs, and outcomes that draw nonprofits toward their desired impact; war on waste seeks economies of scale through mergers and a winnowing of duplication; and watchful eye demands more accessible, easily disseminated information on the internal workings of nonprofits, including administrative and fund-raising ratios that might sort high-performing nonprofits from their poorly performing brethren.

Each also has a different image of what it means to be an effective nonprofit: scientific management sees a sector governed by high standards of excellence; liberation management sees one led forward by careful measurement of success; war on waste sees a sector occupied by fewer, bigger, yet more economical nonprofits; and watchful eye sees a sector that is instantly transparent to the public. The images are not mutually exclusive—one can easily imagine an organization that is simultaneously transparent and outcomes oriented. Nevertheless, the four reform philosophies lead down different pathways toward excellence. Scientific management starts with checklists and self-study, liberation management with strategic planning and measurement, war on waste with a focus on efficiency, and watchful eye with a view toward greater openness and sunshine.

## The Knowledge Gap

The primary reason these tides come and go is that there is little or no evidence on what works and why. Even the private sector has mixed information on the success rates of celebrated reforms such as reengineering, which is designed to reduce duplication, remove needless steps, reduce error rates, and streamline production. As one study of *Fortune 1000* companies shows, the success rate for "radical" corporate reengineering is 20–50 percent, the satisfaction rate among 350 selected executives is 16 percent, the success rate for 600 large North American and European firms that pursued time reductions and productivity increase is 75 percent, the success rate among 166 U.S. and European firms is 27 percent, and the success rate among 75 North American companies is 23 percent.[8]

The same pattern holds for other efforts at change in the private sector. Total quality management has a success rate of 23–39 percent; mergers and acquisitions, 27–80 percent; downsizing, 19 percent; efforts to change organizational culture, 10–32 percent; software development, 16–33 percent; and new computer systems, 17–24 percent. Some other findings are a 16 percent "fully successful" rate (meaning on time, on budget, and fully functional) for 7,500 software projects, 19 percent success in achieving savings and productivity gains for 1,000 downsized companies, 50 percent success among 135 companies that attempted "massive restructuring," and 17 percent success among 30 North American companies that attempted to implement a new computer system.

Not surprisingly, recent studies of reform efforts in nonprofits show similar disappointments. According to a review of 66 separate studies of strategic planning, the link between planning and organizational success is weak at best. Research on how plans are made "has been narrow, concerned with the adoption and use of formal strategic planning rather than broader questions of strategic decision-making processes." Furthermore, research on the implementation of actual plans has virtually ignored "the impact on performance," while the literature on the content of strategic plans has been "silent on the link between particular strategies and measures of performance." And "despite the wealth of research, performance has received scant attention. Whereas research on formulation addresses performance more than research either on content or implementation, what happens between the formulation of strategy and organizational performance is essentially a black box."[9]

Even when researchers arrive at a significant finding, it is often to confirm the lack of a relationship. As has been convincingly demonstrated in
a study of 2,367 nonprofits over ten years with a database containing
23,670 observations, improvements in efficiency are *not* related to higher
charitable giving from foundations: "Nonprofits that position themselves
as cost efficient—reporting low administrative to program expense
ratios—fared no better over time than less efficient appearing organizations in the market for contributions." The far better predictors of success
are how much each nonprofit spends on fund-raising and its overall size.
In other words, nonprofits that are bigger to begin with and spend more
on fund-raising reap higher contributions. Even if it is acknowledged that
administrative cost ratios are notoriously flawed as a measure of true
overhead expenditures and that contributions are only one measure of
performance, efficiency just does not seem to matter to an organization's
success. It has been found that spending more money on fund-raising is a
better strategy for increasing revenues than playing games to make
administrative costs look lower than they truly are.[10]

Management improvement is not just a pathway to higher contributions, however, if it has ever been that at all. For most nonprofits, it
should be first and foremost a pathway to higher mission performance.
For some, it is also a route to self-generated revenues and less depen-
dence. Whether contributors notice the performance is virtually irrelevant to its value to the sector.

## The Infrastructure of Effectiveness

Unfortunately, the effectiveness of the organizational infrastructure
remains weak. Although there have been management support organizations since the 1970s, the field is still building its basic infrastructure,
whether in the form of grantmaking alliances, databases, or consulting
capacity.

The movement for organizational effectiveness suffers from two related
problems. First, there is no commonly understood definition of "organizational effectiveness." Though powerful, the term is also problematic: "It
is powerful in the sense that it represents a useful tool for critically evaluating and enhancing the work of organizations; it is problematic in the
sense that it can mean different things to different people and there exist
many alternative ways of measuring organizational effectiveness."[11]

Second and equally debilitating, there is no commonly accepted wisdom on what might actually help nonprofits improve performance. Even

if a nonprofit wanted to respond to the heightened scrutiny and expectations of today, the field does not have good measurements of what interventions work under which circumstances: "All capacity-building programs have a common purpose—to develop an effective organization that delivers high quality programs and services efficiently and adjusts to both internal and external threats and opportunities so that the organization remains healthy over the longer term."[12]

Yet capacity building is just as difficult to define as organizational effectiveness. Some observers sort capacity building into at least two broad approaches: a focused approach characterized by short-term thinking and the implementation of new systems, and a development approach characterized by longer-term engagement around organizational change. In turn, those two broad approaches contain dozens, if not hundreds, of applications, from training programs to strategic planning, board development, management systems, leadership recruitment, organization restructuring, and fund-raising, each of which can be sorted again by cost, durability, portability, and impact.

Nonprofit boards are a perfect case in point. In theory, better boards should lead to better nonprofits, and more meetings of better boards should lead to even better nonprofits. That is certainly the idea behind most calls for board development.

Once again, however, there is little research to prove the point, and even less to show just how to build a better board. Board effectiveness is almost certainly related to nonprofit effectiveness, the question being how? And in what direction? Just what is an effective board anyway? One that meets a minimum of four times a year, as the Maryland Association of Nonprofit Organizations recommends? One that has prestigious members? And do better boards build higher-performing nonprofits? Or do higher-performing nonprofits attract better boards? The answers are unclear. The same questions surround a host of recent recommendations for improvement, including strategic planning, outcome measurement, and the use of correct management practices.[13]

All in all, the knowledge base offers few lessons to the nonprofit that wants to reengineer or a sector that needs to continually improve. As one nonprofit consultant told our research team last summer, "Researchers tend to like to study problems and practitioners have to solve them; researchers like to write in academic terms and practitioners like very concrete, pragmatic language. Even where the research does exist,

I don't think it's filtering down to people who are running the organizations." It is a sobering prospect for any nonprofit awakened by the call to action.

## Finding Pathways to Excellence

Constructing a clear pathway to higher nonprofit performance is no small task, but several organizations are most certainly trying. The Maryland Association of Nonprofit Organizations is doing so through its Standards of Excellence program, a code of conduct based on "honesty, integrity, fairness, respect, trust, responsibility, and accountability in nonprofit program operations, governance, human resources, financial management and fundraising." The code is composed of fifty-five specific standards, addressing everything from board governance and human resources to financial management, fund-raising, and information technology.

The Maryland association is not alone in setting standards. The Minnesota Council of Nonprofits has its own code of conduct, composed of eighty-eight separate standards, with a much heavier emphasis on nonprofit-ness through core values and behavior. Although the Maryland standards include counsel under the heading "Legal Compliance and Accountability" that Minnesota's do not, the Minnesota standards are much more detailed on basic issues of diversity, accessibility, social justice, information systems, partnership/alliance objectives, and structures (see table 2-1 for a comparison of the two sets of standards).

What makes the Maryland program unique is its voluntary certification program, under which individual nonprofits can seek the association's "seal of excellence" by proving compliance with the standards through a peer-review process involving a written application and site review by an assessment team. In theory, the seal of excellence should improve the odds of funding from the 85 percent of Maryland residents who reported that such a seal would be an important factor in making giving decisions.

The program is also notable for its hoped-for national reach. With a $900,000 grant from the Carnegie Corporation in New York and another $400,000 from Atlantic Philanthropies, the Maryland association is expanding the program to Delaware, north Louisiana, North Carolina, Ohio, and Pennsylvania.

# Table 2-1. Comparing Standards

## Maryland Association of Nonprofit Organizations

Nonprofits are founded for the public good and operate to accomplish a stated purpose through specific program activities. A nonprofit should have a well-defined mission, and its programs should effectively and efficiently work toward achieving that mission. Nonprofits have an obligation to ensure program effectiveness and to devote the resources of the organization to achieving its stated purpose.

### Mission

The organization's purpose, as defined and approved by the board of directors, should be formally and specifically stated. The organization's activities should be consistent with its stated purpose.

### Organizational evaluation

A nonprofit should periodically revisit its mission to determine if the need for its programs continues to exist. The organization should evaluate whether the mission needs to be modified to reflect societal changes, its current programs should be revised or discontinued, or new programs need to be developed.

## Minnesota Council of Nonprofits

A nonprofit is founded for public benefit and operates to accomplish a well-defined, articulated mission. Its programs effectively and efficiently work toward achieving that mission and it is committed to continuous quality improvement. Based on the values of quality, responsibility, and accountability, nonprofit board members, volunteers, and employees act in the best interest of achieving the organization's mission at all times.

### Mission

A nonprofit's purpose (the answer to the question, "Why?" as defined and approved by the board of directors) should be formally stated in writing. The organization's activities should be consistent with its stated purpose.

A nonprofit should, at least biennially, revisit its mission to determine if the need for its services continues to exist. The organization should evaluate whether the mission needs to be modified to reflect societal changes; whether the organization's current programs should be revised or discontinued in light of the existing or newly defined mission; or whether new services need to be developed.

A nonprofit should have defined replicable procedures in place for evaluating (both qualitatively and quantitatively) its processes and outcomes in relation to its mission. These procedures should address the efficiency and cost-effectiveness of processes and outcomes.

### Program Service and Quality

A nonprofit should act with the utmost professionalism and treat all persons equally and with respect.

*Program evaluation*

A nonprofit should have defined, cost-effective procedures for evaluating, both qualitatively and quantitatively, its programs and projects in relation to its mission. These procedures should address programmatic efficiency and effectiveness, the relationship of these impacts to the cost of achieving them, and the outcomes for program participants.

Evaluations should be candid, be used to strengthen the effectiveness of the organization and, when necessary, be used to make programmatic changes.

A nonprofit should regularly monitor the satisfaction of service participants as well as other parts of the organization's constituencies and provide a grievance procedure to address complaints.

A nonprofit should practice continuous quality improvement that includes evaluation and tracking of information.

*Values*

A nonprofit should act with integrity, openness, and honesty in all relationships, dealings, and transactions. A nonprofit should strive to earn and convey trust through integrity, openness, and honesty.

A nonprofit should keep faith with the public trust through efficient, cost-effective, and compassionate stewardship of resources. A nonprofit should be mindful that its mission is accomplished through the generosity of others.

A nonprofit should ensure that policies and procedures of human relations are legally grounded, of high quality, and respectful of the dignity and rights of individuals.

*Commitment to diversity, accessibility, and social justice*

A nonprofit should respect all people's race, religion, ethnicity, gender, age, socio-economic status, sexual orientation, and ability and should not allow differences to affect a person's opportunities.

A nonprofit's board, staff, volunteers, and contractors should reflect the diversity of the organization's constituencies and the broader community.

A nonprofit should conduct its work in facilities that allow reasonable access to persons of all ability levels.

A nonprofit should act in ways that further the equality of opportunity among individuals and communities.

A nonprofit should act in ways that promote a sustainable environment.

## The Practically Perfect Nonprofit

What makes the two programs similar is a desire to describe the core characteristics of a high-performing nonprofit organization, and to do so from inside the sector. The standards are designed to pull individual organizations toward a more hopeful future in which nonprofit-like organizations focus on the public good through mission-centered work and programmatic effectiveness. The standards describe a nonprofit that is practically perfect in every way, rather like Mary Poppins.

At least in Minnesota, the high-performing nonprofit should spend 70 percent of its revenue on programs, use industry-based surveys to set the overall compensation policy, have written policies and procedures governing the work and actions of employees and volunteers, provide quarterly financial reports, have written policies on everything from purchasing practices to expense accounts, respect the privacy of donors, and only use the services of professional fund-raisers registered with the state attorney general. It should also build information systems that provide timely, accurate, and relevant information; invest, where feasible, in telecommunications equipment that enhances its ability to achieve its mission; engage in collaborative efforts "if and when such actions enhance its programmatic objectives and prevent, reduce, or eliminate duplication of services"; and encourage voting and citizen participation in local, state, and federal elections.

Jon Pratt and Peter Berns, the deeply committed executive directors of the Minnesota and Maryland associations, respectively, would almost certainly argue that the standards are not about finding perfection, but about encouraging nonprofits to aspire to higher performance. Nonprofits do not have to meet all the standards to win the Maryland seal of excellence, but they must meet most, and must be moving forward on all fronts.

Much as one can admire the effort to describe the practically perfect nonprofit, many board members, executive directors, and funders rightly wonder whether there is any leverage point that might trigger an inexorable process of improvement. Where does one begin in building the high-performing nonprofit? The board? The information system? The phones?

## Research Methodology

Although the standards must obviously cover important things, a more important question here is how poorly performing nonprofits can move toward higher performance, and how high performers can sustain that performance across the crises, fads, and uncertainties over time. The first challenge is to find enough high performers to answer this question. The growing list of award programs such as the Peter F. Drucker Award for Nonprofit Innovation or the John W. Gardner Leadership Award offers a possible source of names, but many of these programs are so new that they have not generated enough winners to build a sample.[14] Though the oldest, the Drucker Award has had just nineteen winners since 1991, while the Gardner Award focuses on leadership, not organizations.

The perspective of high performance presented in the following pages is based on a very different methodology. The project started in early 2001 with a random-sample telephone survey conducted by Princeton Survey Research Associates of 250 opinion leaders in the organizational effectiveness movement. The sample was drawn from the membership lists of Grantmakers for Effective Organizations (GEO), the Association for Research on Nonprofit and Voluntary Action (ARNOVA), and the Alliance for Nonprofit Management. Of the 250, 85 were from GEO, 80 from ARNOVA, and 85 from the Alliance for Nonprofit Management. Although the combined membership of the three groups totaled only 1,324 names, these are the grantmakers, scholars, and consultants who are most familiar with the characteristics of high-performing nonprofits and pathways to improvement. Their responses to the structured questionnaire are presented in appendix A.

The sample was randomly drawn to ensure that each professional association mentioned above would be represented. The overall response rate was 70 percent. For results based on the total sample, one can say with 95 percent confidence that the error attributable to sampling and other random effects is within approximately plus or minus six percentage points. In addition to sampling error, the wording of questions and practical difficulties in conducting telephone surveys can introduce error or bias into the findings. Hence the structured interviews were followed by hour-long, semistructured interviews with twenty-five respondents to provide added texture and insight to the analysis.

There are two risks in using this methodology. First, it is entirely possible that the opinion leaders simply do not know enough about nonprofit operations to answer the core research question, let alone have enough contact with actual organizations to identify true high performers. Opinion leaders though they certainly are, one simply cannot know whether their opinions of what works in which nonprofits are based on hunch, real experience, or the latest press reports. Second, the sample is almost certainly biased to think of high performance more in organizational rather than programmatic terms.

The opinion leaders were asked about more than just characteristics of high performance and starting points for change, however. They were also asked to identify the names of the two or three organizations that most closely fit the idea of a high-performing organization. This "snowball" yielded a list of 490 exemplary nonprofits, of which 250 were selected for further study. This final sample of 250 included well-known national nonprofits such as the San Francisco Aids Foundation, Big Brothers and Big Sisters of America, the Girl Scouts of America, the Nature Conservancy, Habitat for Humanity, Bread for the World, the Center on Budget and Policy Priorities, CARE, the Big Apple Circus, Public Agenda, the American Friends Service Committee, as well as a host of local organizations such as the Tree Musketeers of Los Angeles, the Pacific Repertory Theater of Carmel, Project for Pride in Living of Minneapolis, Friends of the Chicago River and the Heartland Alliance of Chicago, the Asian and Pacific Islander Wellness Center of San Francisco, the Fayetteville Museum of Art, Parenthood of Rhode Island, the Central Virginia Food Bank, the Henry Street Settlement in New York City, and the Rocky Mountain Youth Corps of Taos, New Mexico.

The executive directors of all 250 organizations were contacted in the summer of 2001 for a telephone survey built around many of the same questions asked of the opinion leaders. Of the 250 executives who eventually responded, 201 were chief executives, 29 were vice presidents or chief operating officers, and 19 were directors of communications, program operations, development, and so forth. Their responses to the structured questionnaire are presented in appendix B. The response rate for this companion study was 60 percent. For results based on the total sample, one can say with 95 percent confidence that the error attributable to sampling and other random effects is within approximately plus or minus six percentage points.

As in the survey of opinion leaders, sampling error, the wording of questions, and practical difficulties in conducting telephone surveys can introduce error or bias into the findings. Structured interviews were again followed by deeper, hour-long conversations with a subset of twenty-five respondents to provide texture and explanation for some of the findings.

There are two risks in using these reputational leaders for insights into the characteristics of high performance. First, having been identified by funders, scholars, and consultants as high performers, the executives of these organizations had ample incentive to present themselves in a favorable light. It is entirely possible, therefore, that they overstated the positive aspects of their external relationships, internal structure, leadership, and management systems and understated the negative ones. Second, it is also possible that these leaders overstated the importance of leadership to high performance. Although the questionnaire was designed to minimize self-aggrandizing, leaders can be expected to celebrate leadership because they are, well, leaders themselves.

Together, the two sets of interviews provide a portrait of the high-performing nonprofit at two levels: from the distant perspective of the grantmaker, scholar, and consultant, and from the front-lines of reputational high performers. Although there are biases in all methodologies, the following analysis suggests that there are, indeed, shared characteristics of high-performing nonprofits and some lessons that poorly performing nonprofits can use in moving toward more nonprofit-like behavior.[15]

## Conclusion

The most important point to emphasize before moving to the survey data is that there is no single pathway to excellence. There appear to be multiple starting points for improvement, several general strategies for growth, and a menu of characteristics that nonprofits can draw upon as target destinations for building capacity. Nonprofits can achieve and sustain high performance without being practically perfect in every way. High performers build upon their assets, be it strong boards, motivated staff, smart leaders, rigorous evaluation, effective fund-raising, or innovative programs.

This does not mean nonprofits can do just about anything and expect to improve. High performance can only be achieved and sustained if an organization knows why it exists, who it serves, and when it is successful. It hardly makes sense to start the journey toward high performance if doing so makes no difference to any one or any thing outside the organization.

## CHAPTER THREE

# Views from a Distance

*"We meet them where they're at."*

The phrase comes as close to a core commandment of capacity building as the nonprofit sector gets. Capacity builders and funders have long believed that the clients should make the decision about what they do to increase effectiveness. Unfortunately, "meeting nonprofits where they're at" often gets translated into "meeting nonprofits wherever they happen to be." Lacking a basic theory about what might work when, where, and how over an organization's life span, capacity builders have had little choice but to offer menus of possible interventions from which their clients or grantees can pick and choose regardless of the potential for success, including the latest fads coming out of the governmental and private sectors.

Nothing could be less helpful as the nonprofit sector answers the call to higher performance. Although some interventions will work, whether because of good luck or random probability, the sector wastes too much of its precious time and energy on interventions that come too early or late in an organization's life. The result is needless motion, wasted effort, ongoing disappointment, and a lingering sense that the nonprofit sector just cannot quite get its act together when it comes to organizational effectiveness.

## Defining Terms

The place to begin the search for high-performing nonprofits is to define the term "organizational effectiveness." After all, it is the stem cell, so to speak, of the broad movement to strengthen an entire sector and is driving a significant amount of funding for a host of capacity-building interventions. Unfortunately, even the leaders of the organizational effectiveness movement seem uncertain about what the term means. When asked what "organizational effectiveness" meant to them, the 250 respondents provided a range of answers. "Using limited resources for the most product impact or managing limited resources to produce the greatest impact," said one. "Doing what they say and staying true to their mission," said another. "Achieving the organization's goal at the least possible expense," said yet another. Still others commented: "How efficient they are, how well they use their resources, and the degree of internal transparency and openness in the organization regarding decisionmaking." "Having solid infrastructure running smoothly to achieve the outcome." "It's a whole range of things: Anything from efficient practices to satisfaction with constituents to the absence of laws in an organization." "It means programs that have a genuine impact in the community." "Define it as stable organizations where revenue meets and ideally exceeds expenses over the long term."

Despite the variety, some common themes run through the answers. Almost half of the respondents referred to "mission" at some point, while three in five equated effectiveness with being focused on or accomplishing a mission or goals. Another quarter defined effective in management terms, while just 4 percent mentioned good leadership.

These respondents may be experts in management improvement, but they clearly believe that programmatic impact is the sine qua non of high performance. Hence 44 percent strongly agreed that an organization can be very well managed and still not achieve its program goals, while 27 percent strongly agreed that an organization can be very effective in achieving its program goals but not be well managed.

The community agrees that good management is a necessary, but not sufficient, requirement for program impact. As table 3-1 shows, 58 percent of the respondents either strongly or somewhat agreed with both statements, confirming the notion that being well managed is not an end in itself. At least for the opinion leaders, there appear to be plenty of well-managed nonprofits that do not make a programmatic difference, and plenty of organizations that make a programmatic difference in spite of poor management.

The organizational effectiveness movement is rooted in both external and internal pressure. Even as the government, funders, and watchdogs

**Table 3-1. *Agreeing with Contradictions*[a]**

Percent

| An organization can be very effective in achieving its program goals but not be well managed | An organization can be very well managed and still not achieve its program goals | | | |
|---|---|---|---|---|
| | Strongly agree | Somewhat agree | Somewhat disagree | Strongly disagree |
| Strongly agree | 15 | 20 | 5 | 4 |
| Somewhat agree | 9 | 14 | 9 | 4 |
| Somewhat disagree | 1 | 4 | 4 | 2 |
| Strongly disagree | 2 | 4 | 2 | 2 |

a. N = 247.

demand greater accountability, many nonprofit organizations are already trying to become more nonprofit-like by raising the bar on their own performance. Asked why people are talking about organizational effectiveness, the longer conversations with twenty-five of the opinion leaders revealed a mix of reasons for the increased interest in effectiveness. Survival was at the top of the list. "I think the reason more people are talking about organizational effectiveness is that we are having to do more with less," said one member of the Alliance for Nonprofit Management. "We are having to be more effective in order to stay alive. I also think the funders have come around to recognize that investing in the overall effectiveness of an organization is critical. So, of course, when the funding community became extremely interested in outcomes, the nonprofit community became extremely interested in outcomes. At least in a superficial way."[1]

A GEO member also pointed to funding pressure. "I am sure nonprofits are feeling it from their boards, and they are certainly feeling it from their funders . . . like us; I know they are feeling it from us. They feel it from the United Way, which has put a big effort into accountability measures." "Nonprofits are trying to get more and more done with fewer resources," an alliance member agreed. "They are strapped, they are really stretched thin and they have to figure out which of their programs are really making a difference and which aren't." A second alliance member put it more bluntly: "Grantmakers are running scared because the question is being asked of them and the tendency is to always turn around and ask it of us."

At least in these interviews, the push for accountability was evident well before September 11. As an ARNOVA member noted, "The sector's gotten a lot more attention in the past ten years and people are becoming more educated on what they do and they want to hold organizations accountable for the money and the tax benefits. I think that effectiveness is one of the ways that the public ensures that nonprofits are doing what they should be doing." But not all of the accountability comes from outside the organization. "We owe it to the American public and to ourselves to do the best possible jobs," said a GEO member. "That is a heavier accountability to me than the accountability of the marketplace. It doesn't say, 'Well, we don't like your product this week, so you're going out of business.' It says instead that nonprofits have a moral responsibility, an ethical responsibility to do your jobs well."

Asked where the pressure is coming from, the vast majority of these respondents talked about foundations, boards, and government. "We're under increased scrutiny from our own donors to answer the question about what difference we make," said a GEO community foundation member. "That's a perfectly good question. Our own boards are asking that, too. Whether you have a lot of restricted money or a lot of unrestricted, you want to make sure you are getting good value for the investments. This is no longer an armchair kind of good-old-boy-clubby industry. We are trying very hard to apply business models and have reasonable expectations for returns on the money we send out."

Boards are also putting greater pressure on their own organizations. As an ARNOVA member argued, "We used to have an awful lot of business types who got put on our boards to represent this company or that bank. That still occurs some, but more and more you are getting folks coming on these boards who run their own businesses. So they look at things from the perspective of what they had to do to spin off their own business."

The government is becoming more aggressive about effectiveness, too. "There is a lot of evidence that state agencies have developed some fairly sophisticated ways of monitoring protocol, performance, and very specific procedures for ensuring that contractors are performing as expected," said an ARNOVA member. "That's the price for taking money from government."

"Everyone is speeding up," said a GEO member of the mounting pressure. "And these people who sit on boards expect and demand these organizations to be more effective. You hear these business people talking about duplication of services and having organizations collaborate or even consolidate their operations. There's a McDonald's on every street corner and a gasoline station across the street. But under their idea, there should be just one gas station in town and we should all go to it."

Yet for every comment against winnowing, there was one in favor of downsizing. "The survival of the fittest kicks in at some level," another GEO member said. "If you have three Meals on Wheels programs operating within 20 miles of each other, there is some duplication and it's unnecessary. In some cases, funders have insisted on mergers or paid for analysis. But in most cases it's the agencies themselves realizing that the time is right." A third GEO member agreed: "A certain amount of failure is a healthy thing. I don't think we should describe every failure or a certain number of failures as a tragedy."

Not all of the pressure was external, however. At least some respondents talked about the generational shift toward younger, more business-oriented nonprofit executives. "I call it for-profit chauvinism," another ARNOVA member said of the "Gen X business folks." "They are convinced that if nonprofits ran in a more business-like manner, they would be more effective. They are coming into the nonprofit job with more business acumen, a finance background or accounting background."

Others talked about the internal pressure to do good. "I think staffs want to be more effective," said an ARNOVA member. "They believe in the cause and they want to make sure that things happen that move the organization forward." A GEO member focused on professional expectations. "For larger organizations, the pressure comes from their own size, complexity, and national connections—in other words, the professional expectations at their national level." A second GEO member summed up the pressure in similar terms, with a bit of war on waste thrown in:

> There is this growing sense that being nonprofit is a profession. There is a lot more coverage of nonprofit activity, too. Twenty-five years ago, nonprofits never made the front page of the paper. That's all changed. I can't remember when the United Way scandal hit— seems like only yesterday. But it wasn't that many years ago that a lot of stuff was either hidden from public view or not reported. Nonprofits now understand that they have a great deal of account-

ability to their donors and to the community, and some actually believe that they are going to hang together or hang separately.

As for the words that best describe high-performing organizations, the full sample of opinion leaders carried a relatively clean image of high performance rooted more in principle than entrepreneurship. Seventy-six percent of the respondents said the word "principled" described high-performing organizations very well, followed by "resilient" at 72 percent, "innovative" at 64 percent, "collaborative" at 51 percent, "rigorous" at 40 percent, and "entrepreneurial" at 37 percent.

The three groups of opinion leaders were not in complete agreement here. Although all three groups agreed on the importance of principles, the GEO members put greater emphasis on rigor than their peers, ARNOVA members put less emphasis on innovation and resilience than their peers, and alliance members put greater emphasis on entrepreneurship than their peers. The pattern fits with what one might expect from the three groups. The GEO members are trained to look for rigor as part of the due diligence involved in grantmaking, ARNOVA members have the natural skepticism about buzz words like "innovative," while the alliance members might favor the word "entrepreneurial" because it fits with the strategic organizations that are more likely to consume technical assistance.

## The Demographics of High Performance

No matter where they sit, the opinion leaders stay in touch with the front lines. On average, they worked with 96 nonprofits in 2000; alliance members worked with 139, GEO members with 104, and ARNOVA members with 42. Of these organizations, the opinion leaders said they knew 22 well, or roughly a fifth, with GEO members leading the group this time at 28, followed by alliance members at 26, and ARNOVA members at 15. Only 1 percent of the entire sample said they knew fewer than 10 nonprofits well.

Given this range of contact, it is not surprising that the opinion leaders have a mixed view of nonprofit performance. On the one hand, more than three-quarters (77 percent) strongly or somewhat agreed that nonprofits are better managed today than they were five years ago. On the other hand, only 21 percent said that most of the nonprofits they know well are high-performing, while 48 percent said some, and 30 percent said only a few. If nonprofits are better managed than they were five years ago, the results are not yet showing up in the number of high performers.

All high-performing nonprofits are not the same, however. Respondents were more likely to see high performance in three settings: (1) in organizations with a budget between $500,000 and $10 million, (2) in organizations that are middle-aged (seven to fifteen years old) or older (older than fifteen), and (3) in organizations that experienced rapid or moderate growth over the past five years. Respondents saw less high performance in organizations that were very small or very large, and in organizations that were very young, and saw no high performers in organizations that had experienced moderate or rapid declines in growth.

It is hard to know exactly what these data mean, since they challenge the conventional wisdom that midsize, middle-aged organizations are among the toughest to manage. It could just be that these respondents only know a certain size of organization well. Big organizations such as the Red Cross, Boys and Girls Clubs, and YMCA/YWCA may be so well managed and funded that they rarely get in touch with GEO, ARNOVA, and alliance members. It may also be that very small organizations are so underfunded and overstressed that they move through the sector unnoticed.

One must then ask whether this is the true demography of high performance or just the demography of the high performance known to these opinion leaders. One way to answer this question is to look back at the number of high performers each respondent said they knew well.

Respondents who said most of the organizations they knew were high performers knew an average of just thirteen organizations well, while respondents who characterized only a few of the organizations they knew as high performers knew an average of twenty organizations well. As one gets to know the sector well, the number of high performers declines as a percentage but rises as an absolute. And as the number rises as an absolute, the potential spread of high performance across different demographic categories is also likely to spread.

As if to prove the point, opinion leaders who knew more nonprofits well were also less likely to say that management has improved. Thus 42 percent who saw high performance among most of the nonprofits they knew well also said most nonprofits are better managed today than they were five years ago, compared with just 22 percent of their peers. Familiarity does not breed contempt per se, but it does breed a sense that high performance is possible in many settings, but rare nonetheless. It is a hopeful, but sobering theme.

The opinion leaders as a whole also saw a different kind of leader at the top of the high-performing nonprofits they knew. Only 5 percent said the founding director was still at most of the high-performing organizations they knew. Headed by a founder or not, high performers had experienced leaders at the helm. Only 10 percent said that the leaders of most high-performing organizations had been in their position for less than five years, and 66 percent said most of the high performers had leaders who had been in the nonprofit sector most of their careers. Only 8 percent said that most had leaders with any private sector experience at all. Some of these demographic impressions are at odds with the realities found among the 250 high performing organizations actually contacted, 41 percent of which still had their founding director.

## Perceived States of Being Nonprofit-like

Given the emphasis on standards of excellence, it is important to determine whether high-performing nonprofits share any characteristics that might be copied by poorly performing nonprofits. It must first be acknowledged, however, that this research cannot yield a set of absolutes, particularly given the absence of a control group of poor performers against which to compare the lessons of high performance. Because this study focused foremost on the search for high performers, the best one can do is generate what I have called *preferred states of organizational being*.

All things being equal, one could argue, organizations should be led by dedicated boards and thoughtful, strategic leaders. It would be difficult to argue otherwise. Yet many organizations, including some of the 250 high performers, are almost certainly led by underengaged boards and poorly trained leaders. Lacking a control group of poor performers against which to judge the high performers, however, one can only say that it is probably better to have smart boards and leaders than not. So, too, for the rest of the characteristics found in the four broad categories of organizational life discussed next: (1) external relationships, (2) internal structure, (3) leadership, and (4) internal management systems.[2]

### External Relationships

Nonprofits can only do so much about the world in which they exist. Although some rightly argue that they could do more to influence the environment through political and social advocacy, many organizations take the environment as a given and focus their attention on internal structure, leadership, and systems as the leverage points for improvement. Beyond strengthening their fund-raising, many nonprofits simply believe the world is unchangeable.

The opinion leaders and executives interviewed for this study believe quite differently. They see high performance as rooted at least in part in aggressive interaction with the outside world. Simply stated, high-performing nonprofits have their faces turned to the outside world, exposing themselves to the winds of change, competition, and turbulence. For good or ill, they refuse to hunker down against the winds.

According to the opinion leaders, most of the high-performing nonprofits manage the external environment in similar ways: they collaborate, make money, diversify, and measure results. At least half of the opinion leaders identified these characteristics among most of the high-performing nonprofits they knew well.

—*Collaborate*. Although collaboration can mean everything from sharing information to sharing services and strategic alliances, 70 percent of the opinion leaders reported that high performers actively collaborate with other organizations. Alliance members were less likely to see the pattern than their peers, perhaps because they see some partnerships that exist in name only.

—*Make Money*. Despite their refusal to link the word "entrepreneurial" with high performance, 68 percent of the opinion leaders said that most of the high performers they knew generate at least some unrestricted income. The GEO and ARNOVA members were less likely to see the characteristic, perhaps because high-performing nonprofits have some incentive to hide this capacity from the outside world, lest it be used as a reason to reduce operating support.

—*Diversify*. Almost two-thirds of the opinion leaders said most of the high performers they knew have a diversified funding base. The GEO members were somewhat more likely to endorse the characteristic, in part because diversification comes as close to a core concept of Grantmaking 101 as having clean financial audits.

—*Measure*. Just over half of the opinion leaders said most high performers measure the results or outcomes of what they do. Although some experts might argue that this is a characteristic of internal management, measurement forces the organization to look outside itself for insights on its performance and is part of being honest and rigorous in determining when it is successful. Alliance members were slightly less likely to emphasize this characteristic, again perhaps because they may be closer to the substance of measurement.

The opinion leaders were less likely to say that the high performers they knew well regularly survey their clients regarding programs and services. Only 41 percent said they saw such surveys in most of the high performers they knew, with no statistical differences among the three groups. Interestingly, 92 percent of the high-performing nonprofits contacted in the second survey said they use client surveys to a large or fair extent, suggesting another disconnect between what outsiders see and what high-performing nonprofits actually do. It is quite possible that high performers simply do not share this kind of information with their funders.

Just because opinion leaders saw these characteristics does not mean most of the high performers were doing them well. In the longer interviews, respondents were particularly skeptical about nonprofits' attitudes toward outcomes measurement. "I think nonprofits are aware that these things are in the wind or that they are part of a funder's decisionmaking," said one GEO member. "But I don't think they believe we take it seriously yet. They have their heads in the sand because the time has come when more and more funders will be expecting clearly measurable results and business plans that make sense. We're raising our expectations of the nonprofits and I don't think they think we're serious about it yet." A second GEO member agreed: "I've certainly seen outcomes measurement as a distraction. Folks panic instead of viewing it as a management tool. 'How do I look at my programs and see where I could do a better job?' 'How do I get the information that's going to tell me that this program is working and this one needs to be reassessed?' Those are the critical questions of today."

At the same time, the opinion leaders did not see the outside world as being a particularly difficult place for high-performing nonprofits to manage. Only 23 percent said the environment of most of the high performers they knew is turbulent, and only 10 percent characterized it as heavily regulated. Rather, most of the opinion leaders think the environment is best described as competitive. "I think the reason more people are talking about organization effectiveness is that, just like every other form of business, we are having to do more with less," said an alliance member. "Attract clients, provide good service, because, whether we are nonprofits or for-profits, airline tickets cost the same. Human resources are costing more and more because it is a seller's market. We not only have to be more effective at offering money, but we have to be more attractive places to work." Another alliance member focused on the competition created as the private sector moves into nontraditional arenas reserved for nonprofit and faith-based organizations: "With new players in the field, there is a kind of a circling the wagons in response."

### Internal Structure

"Bureaucracy" has to be one of the least used terms in the nonprofit sector. According to conventional wisdom, most nonprofits are flat, team-oriented organizations that have few barriers between units and give staff the authority to make routine decisions on their own. Although there are certainly exceptions to this wisdom in the form of the large, highly formalized bureaucracies at national organizations such as the Salvation Army, which was built on a military model, most nonprofits are viewed as too small to generate the hierarchies that are so familiar in the government and the corporate world.

Nonprofits still must pay attention to organizational structure, however, if only to avoid the needless clutter that accumulates in most organizations as they age. Opinion leaders interviewed for this report found five common organizational characteristics in the high-performing nonprofits:

—*Exploit technology.* Although nonprofits may not have state-of-the-art or even near-state-of-the-art technologies, 74 percent of the opinion leaders said most high performers use information technology such as e-mail and the Internet to enhance performance. Although alliance members were significantly more likely than GEO and ARNOVA members to identify this characteristic, in all three subsamples technology was essential to high performance.

—*Give staff the authority to do their jobs.* Two-thirds of the opinion leaders saw empowerment, as it is sometimes called, as a common feature of high performance. Doing so is easier recommended than done perhaps, as indicated by the fact that GEO and alliance members were statistically less likely than ARNOVA members to find it among the high performers they knew.

—*Work in teams and give staff the freedom to work together.* If collaboration is good for the outside world, it is also good for the inside world. That is certainly what 55 percent of the opinion leaders saw in the high performers they knew well. There were no statistically significant differences among the three subsamples on giving staff from different parts of the organization the freedom to work together and encouraging them to do so in teams.

—*Stay flat.* Fifty-one percent of the opinion leaders said that most higher performers had few layers of management between the top and bottom of the organization. Given the conventional wisdom about flat, lean nonprofits, this characteristic appears to be more a glass half empty than full. Alliance members were more than ten percentage points less likely than their peers to see the flatness, suggesting that at least some of this finding comes from not seeing nonprofits up close. There may be more nonprofit bureaucracy out there than most observers are willing to admit.

There was also less diversity out there. Only 42 percent said that most high performers had demographically diverse staffs, which was defined in the survey as young and old, male and female, black, Latino, and white.

The focus on technology was particularly clear in the longer interviews. "Nonprofits are frantically trying to figure out how to use technology and trying to get it," said one alliance member. "For many, having two computers would be heaven, let alone creating an interactive website to serve their clients." As one GEO member described another organization, "It is more than just websites. It is interactivity. They can get to documents, personnel information; outside groups can get to what they need. Really cute. They also have an ability for donors to access that information. It might all be smoke and mirrors, but it sure looks good from the outside."

Before turning to the leadership of high-performing organizations, it is important to note the absence of at least one structural characteristic that might enhance performance. Only 30 percent of the opinion leaders said that most of the high-performing nonprofits they knew had rainy-day, or reserve, funds. The GEO members were significantly less likely than ARNOVA and alliance members to notice the characteristic, presumably because nonprofits would hide reserve funds from the outside world. That certainly appears to be the case among the 250 high performers. Only 7 percent of the group said they had no rainy-day fund at all, another 32 percent said they had a small fund, 41 percent a moderate fund, and 19 percent a large fund.

It is also important to note that few of the opinion leaders thought high-performing nonprofits were having trouble retaining quality people. Only 23 percent saw any problems with retaining staff, and even fewer saw a problem in retaining volunteers (18 percent), leaders (12 percent), and board members (6 percent). This hardly means the sector is not facing a demographic problem as its work force ages into retirement, however.

Nor does it mean that opinion leaders and executives discount the impact of good people. It was a point emphasized repeatedly in the long interviews with both sets of respondents. "Nonprofit leaders are only going to be as effective as the people around them," one executive director of a homeless center said. "I want to surround myself with creative, progressive thinkers and with people who can get the job done. I want them to have the ability to reframe issues in new ways." "The main element in high performance is people," said a museum director. "You have to hire people who are mission driven, passionate about their work. Then you have to encourage professional training so they can be learning about what is happening out there to stay current."

One final point: not everyone in these interviews felt that low turnover among board members was such a good thing. Even though only 6 percent said that most high performers were having trouble retaining board members, at least one alliance member saw the low turnover as a problem. "One of the biggest mistakes I've seen is trying to convert lazy board members into gung-ho, active, helpful board members. There is a lot of work that needs to be done on boards. It's a huge waste of time to start the work unless you have some really good people on the board who aren't being used. You shouldn't start if you don't have the right people, or if the assessment says there is a lot of dead wood that will never do anything."

## Leadership

It is impossible to overstate the importance of the leader to the high-performing organization. As an ARNOVA member argued, "Every nonprofit with which I am familiar has either been created or sustained by virtue of having strong leadership." Leadership was seen as the number one, and almost only, place to begin the journey from poor performance to high.

The opinion leaders talked more about *what* successful leaders did than their personal traits. They saw very few charismatic leaders among the high performers, for example. To the extent that opinion leaders talked about charisma, they did so in an entirely negative way. "The organizations that fail in my opinion have a charismatic leader who doesn't let go and can't really do it all," said a GEO member.

Leadership is deeply intertwined with mission. An alliance member focused on the need to say "no": "I see organizations that flounder because they are all over the place trying to be everything to everyone. . . . Actually trying to be everything to every foundation. They are being driven by where the money is." A second alliance member put it in particularly blunt terms:

> Sometimes organizations lose sight of why they exist in the first place. They have these meetings in which nothing really gets discussed. They don't deal with the heart of the organization, but with parliamentary procedure as part of establishing policies about when to use the men's room and when to use the women's room. By that point your organization is dead unless a leader comes along to change it. One of my favorite stories is the "Emperor's New Clothes." I think organizations need to recognize when they are naked. And so they need to keep asking that question, why are we doing this? Is this really necessary? Is this achieving our objectives, whatever they may be? Or are we doing this because Mr. Big Bucks is telling us to do it?

At least for members of GEO, ARNOVA, and the alliance, the key to successful leadership involved a series of practices that allowed the organization to succeed in its external and internal relationships, whether through decent systems, team building, staff development, or good fundraising. In essence, the nonprofit leader must create the conditions for others to succeed as follows:

—*Foster open communications.* Seventy-two percent of the opinion leaders said that most of the high-performing organizations had executives who fostered open communications. The characteristic fits with the earlier findings on collaboration and team building. It is hard to enter into partnerships without at least some level of honesty and nearly impossible to delegate authority downward into the organization without open lines upward.

—*Motivate people.* Seventy percent also said most of the executives knew how to motivate people. Since only 15 percent later said that most high-performing nonprofits linked staff pay to performance, the motivation has to come from focusing on mission.

—*Fund-raise.* Sixty-five percent considered fund-raising a core characteristic of leaders of most high-performing nonprofits Tallied separately, the figures were 69 percent of the GEO and alliance members compared with 56 percent of ARNOVA members.

—*Clarify board/staff relationships.* Even as they reported a high degree of power sharing both within and across nonprofits, 59 percent of the opinion leaders also saw clear lines regarding the respective roles of boards and executives. As the long interviews suggest, boards set the broad policies of the organizations, reinforce the mission, and help raise money but leave the day-to-day operations to the executive director and staff.

—*Embrace participation.* Just over half the respondents said that most of the high performers they knew had leaders who had a participatory style. The numbers varied widely by subsample. Only 40 percent of the GEO members spotted the characteristic, compared with 52 percent of the alliance members and 61 percent of the ARNOVA members. Either the GEO members do not get close enough to see the participatory style, or the ARNOVA members merely assume it.

The longer interviews with the subset of twenty-five opinion leaders suggest that effective nonprofit leaders come with many traits. Some leaders are charismatic, most are not; most are good fund-raisers, some are not; some are good at delegating, most have a participatory style. Some of those traits can be taught; others are intrinsic. "You can teach people to adjust their management style and use situational leadership," said one GEO member. "But I don't think you can teach someone who is not naturally high energy to suddenly find the right vitamins and become a dynamo."

Asked what distinguishes the leaders of high-performing nonprofits, these twenty-five respondents identified thirty-six traits, including interpersonal skills (mentioned by 32 percent); communication skills (28 percent); passion and commitment (24 percent); vision (24 percent); integrity, trust, credibility (20 percent); delegation skills (20 percent); team-building skills (16 percent); willingness to work hard/long hours (16 percent); a focus on mission (16 percent); ability to make hard choices (16 percent); recruiting skills (12 percent); strategic insight (12 percent); consensus-building skills (12 percent); political/community skills (12 percent); and flexibility (8 percent). "There are something like 460 definitions of leadership out there," an ARNOVA member said. "I teach leadership every semester, and even I've stopped counting."

The two traits missing from the list were charisma and risk taking. Only 32 percent of the opinion leaders said the high performers they knew had leaders who could be described as charismatic, and just 41 percent said the high performers had leaders who encourage risk taking. Not surprisingly perhaps, the respondents most likely to see those traits also said most of the organizations they knew well were high performers. After all, organizations led by charismatic leaders are most likely to become known to people who know only a few organizations well.

Whatever the traits, there is no question that leadership plays a significant role in sustaining high performance. "Structure and management are critically important to an organization," an alliance member noted. "But weak leadership leaves the structure and management without direction. I think organizations not only need the modeling that good, strong leadership provides, but they need the centering, if you will, the focus that strong leadership provides. People in the organization need to know that there is someone, or many someones, they can turn to." Another alliance member agreed: "What distinguishes leaders of high-performing organizations? They connect emotionally with the people that they lead. And they create opportunities for others to motivate themselves. They inspire people and help people find inspiration."

An ARNOVA member said essentially the same thing in focusing on relationships: "You are in a perpetual relationship-building model. And therefore, you are not trying to pick fights, throw rocks, or looking for adversaries. You understand that what goes around comes around. So you really try to build bridges and develop relationships in everything you do. You never know when you are going to need one of those or when you're going to walk back that direction. It isn't just put-upon behavior or disingenuous stuff."

### Internal Management Systems

Management systems can be seen as the glue that holds together leaders, structures, and the environment. They are the eyes on the outside world, provide the links between layers and units of the hierarchy, and give leaders and their boards the essential tools for setting priorities, building resilience, and taking risks.

The opinion leaders saw plenty of evidence that systems contribute to high performance but also worried about the fads that are moving through the sector. Many focused specifically on outcomes measurement, which is arguably the hottest trend among funders. The most common concern was simply that nonprofits do not know how to build the systems needed to measure outcomes. "Some organizations just don't know how to do it," said an ARNOVA member, "so it becomes more of a burden than a help. Either they use poor methods or simply make it all up because somebody wants to see their measures." An alliance member echoed the concern. "I'm not sure that many of the foundations or United Ways could even define what outcomes measurement is. I guess I will be honest. I don't know what we are talking about. I don't know what it means. Nothing I read helps me understand what it means. We keep grabbing these panaceas that are supposed to be the answer."

The opinion leaders also worried about the pressure to be more business-like through new systems. "Some people believe that if it's worked in the private sector, it can work in the nonprofit sector," a GEO member remarked. "I think that it's a little bit more individualized than that. Business tools can be useful, but it depends (a) on the tool in question, (b) on the organization in question, and (c) the issue that they're trying to address. It's not a given." An alliance member talked specifically about the pressure to get better at marketing: "I think there is great potential there, but either nonprofits are not really using marketing or they don't know what they are doing. The sector is not built for that."

Despite these concerns, the opinion leaders did see five common characteristics in the systems that high-performing nonprofits use:

—*Use the board*. High-performing nonprofits work their boards hard. Ninety percent of the opinion leaders said that most of the high performers they knew held at least four board meetings a year. At least for the 250 high-performing nonprofits interviewed later, four is the bare minimum: 35 percent said they meet with their boards at least nine times a year.

—*Be clear about responsibility*. More than three-quarters of the opinion leaders said most of the high performers they knew had position descriptions for their staff. It seems reasonable to assume that this characteristic is more a consequence of the demographics of high performance, meaning bigger budgets, than a cause. The bigger the organization gets, the more formalized its structure.

—*Plan for the future*. Seventy-three percent of the opinion leaders said their high performers had strategic plans for the future. Ninety-one percent of the high performers did have strategic plans, two–thirds of which were completed within the last two years.

—*Use data to make decisions*. Despite all the complaints about the difficulty of measurement, 63 percent of the opinion leaders said most of the high performers they knew used data to make informed decisions. The ARNOVA members were significantly more likely than the other two subsamples to see the use of data, perhaps because that is the world in which they work.

*—Invest in training.* Just over half the opinion leaders said most high performers have programs or resources for staff training. There was sharp disagreement among the three groups on this characteristic, however. Only a third of GEO members saw the characteristic, compared with three-fifths of alliance members and two-thirds of ARNOVA members. It could well be that GEO members simply are not close enough to see activity, or that alliance and ARNOVA members see more training going on.

It is important to note the three characteristics that a majority of opinion leaders did *not* see: (1) 47 percent said most of the high performers had an accurate, fast accounting system, (2) 36 percent said most had adequate information technology, and (3) only 15 percent said most linked staff pay to performance. These findings contradict at least one of the characteristics described earlier in this chapter. How can most high performers exploit technology to make decisions when so few have adequate information technology to begin with? It could well be that high performers make do with what they have, meaning not state-of-the-art, not even near-state-of-the-art, systems but whatever old systems they can beg, borrow, or steal.

The lack of adequate systems certainly helps explain the problems with accurate, fast accounting systems, which in turn may help explain the glass nearly half empty on training for staff. "Staff development is the weakest part of the nonprofit world," said one ARNOVA member. We budget virtually none of our operating budgets to training and staff development. We hire people with degrees and do minimal training. If I can find 1 percent in a nonprofit's operating budget for staff development, it is a lot."

The lack of pay-for-performance systems also fits with earlier questions about how leaders motivate staff. There may be position descriptions in the file cabinets, but it is not clear that they matter to pay or other business-like incentives. "Motivation is an area that somewhat mystifies me," said an ARNOVA member. "I have seen some research showing that high-performing individuals only need to be told they're high-performing, and they continue. How an executive director gets to be an effective motivator depends on each person. Some feel comfortable giving out the employee-of-the-month t-shirt; other are more effective using action plans, and giving people goals they need to reach."

Moreover, as one alliance member cautioned, the key person in the organization may not even be a paid staffer. "I once looked at an arts organization in which the person who really kept the place running was the little old lady who ran the gift shop. She made sure everything happened in that organization, and she was a volunteer. I guess if you're in a large organization, you can certainly look at all the people who hold some sort of rank, but you should be aware of the volunteers who are important to the organization."

## Getting Started

It is one thing to list the common characteristics of high-performing nonprofits and quite another to help poorly performing nonprofits start the journey up the developmental spiral that leads from the organic stage of nonprofit life toward the resilience seen in so many high performers. The key is to separate the consequences of high performance, such as a board that is worth convening regularly, from the causes, such as a leader who knows how to fund-raise and make choices.

Therein lies both the potential and frustration of the standards movement. Even if the Maryland and Minnesota standards cover the vast majority of the characteristics of excellent nonprofits, they simply cannot tell what comes first. "This whole movement toward codes and standards of performance is just useless," one alliance member remarked. "It is not about being perfect. It is about ethical decisionmaking and principled reasoning. Organizations should develop their own standards that they are going to measure themselves by. The idea that we can create one that all nonprofits can use is just ludicrous."

### Forced Choices

The simplest way to sort consequence from cause is to ask what poorly performing nonprofits should do to get better. In other words, what should a nonprofit do first to become a high-performing organization: work on becoming well managed or work on increasing its program impacts? Fifty-seven percent said first work on becoming well managed, another 21 percent answered first work on increasing program impacts, and 18 percent said "both."

The biggest statistical difference came between ARNOVA members and their peers. Whereas the GEO and alliance members were almost equal (61 and 64 percent, respectively) in saying nonprofits should first work on becoming well managed, only 46 of the ARNOVA members agreed. At 38 percent, they were almost three times as likely as GEO (12 percent) and alliance (14 percent) members to put their faith in program impacts.

The explanation almost certainly lies in the core commitments of GEO and alliance members to improve management as a neglected focus of nonprofit work. "Many foundations get grant requests that pull on the heart-strings, like helping the cats and dogs at the animal shelter," said one GEO member. "But how can you cuddle up to a new computer system or software? How can you go home and tell your family that 'I really solved some of community's problems today by giving somebody a new phone system'?"

A more sophisticated forced choice involves the four aspects of organizational life: external relationships, internal structure, leadership, and internal management systems. Asked to choose the one area that is most important for a below-average organization to improve first, the opinion leaders were clear. Leadership came in first among 64 percent of the respondents, followed by internal management systems at 17 percent, internal structure at 14 percent, and external relationships at 2 percent.

Having identified the most important starting point for improvement, the 250 opinion leaders were then asked to identify just what change in external relationships, internal structure, leadership, or internal management systems should come first. Their top-ten list is as follows: have a clear understanding with executives and boards about their respective roles (48 respondents, or 19 percent of the total sample, picked this specific step); know how to motivate people (31 respondents, or 12 percent); have a participatory style of management (26 respondents, or 10 percent); have a strategic plan for the future (22 respondents, or 9 percent); foster open communications (17 respondents, or 7 percent); encourage staff to work in teams (10 respondents, or 4 percent); give staff the authority to make routine decisions on their own (8 respondents, or just over 3 percent); have few barriers between organizational units and use data to make decisions (tied at 7 respondents, or just under 3 percent); have few layers of management between the top and bottom of the organization, be a good fund-raiser, encourage risk taking (tied at 5 respondents, or 2 percent).

The list can be sorted into four broad categories by combining recommendations by subject, not area of organizational life. Thirty-three percent of the respondents focused on people as the key starting point, for example, suggesting that below-average performers should start by finding leaders who have a participatory style of management and know how to motivate people, build organizations that encourage staff to work in teams, delegate the authority to make routine decisions, and provide access to training. Another 26 percent emphasized the need to set clear expectations by clarifying board/staff understandings and fostering open communications, while 12 percent stressed strategic thinking through strategic planning and using data to make decisions, and 5 percent targeted different aspects of organizational restructuring by recommending that below-average performers remove barriers between units and flatten their hierarchies to minimize layering.

The fact that external relationships do not appear on this list does not mean these opinion leaders think the external environment is irrelevant. Rather, it may reflect a belief that the external environment is a given that cannot be changed by individual nonprofits, especially ones that are performing poorly. It may also reflect a sense that the outside world is something to be avoided for improving performance. "An awful amount of change comes from the outside world in the form of demands, orders, or screams, and the change it produces is usually unsuccessful," said an ARNOVA member. "In that regard, it might lead one to believe that the external world is somehow irrelevant, which it most certainly is not."

### Why Leadership Comes First

No matter how the answers are assembled, leadership always emerges as the starting point for the journey toward high performance. When asked to explain its prominence in the survey, one ARNOVA member said that it is the answer to every problem: "A slightly less cynical answer is that every one of the things in organizational life is integrally linked to leadership. And in that sense, leadership is at its core about relationships and direction. It's sort of an easy, abstract answer to give." Another ARNOVA seconded the explanation: "We have a very romantic view of leaders, a romantic, heroic view. The problem is that the term means so many different things out there in the world. If anybody can save us, it must be the leaders. People can think of lots of different ways they can improve leadership. So, it's seen as a very big lever."

Whether influenced by romanticism or not, leadership is seen as essential for improvement. "Committed, involved, active, knowledgeable, and aware leadership can overcome a great many faults in the structure of an organization," said an alliance member. Without strong leadership, no

amount of structure is going to take you to organizational effectiveness."
A second alliance member said virtually the same thing: "If you have poor
leadership, your organizational structure will hold up for a while and
pieces of it will work. But without strong leadership, it's going to come
apart. Great leaders inspire by doing, and in doing, improve the organization." A third alliance member summarized the role of leadership in
existential terms:

> An organization is really just a concept. It only exists to the extent
> that there are people who believe it exists. So I mean it's a little exis-
> tential. It's like a neighborhood. Sure you have houses in proximity
> to each other. But it's only when there are certain kinds of bonds
> and interactions going on that it becomes a neighborhood and the
> same is true of organizations. I think leadership is the force that
> makes an organization real.

A GEO member took a more contrary position: "I think this is based
on the notion that people occasionally see a tremendous leader. I think the
fallacy is to assume that there is one right person out there who will rescue the organization, but that does not mean leadership is irrelevant. The
best leaders I know are not charismatic, but inclusive. They lead by example and give people the chance to succeed."

Even though 61 percent of ARNOVA members said leadership was
the most important starting point for change in the telephone surveys,
they were the ones who often dismissed leadership as a shop-worn answer
in the long interviews. It was the GEO and alliance members who saw the
advantages of strong leadership in the long conversations, perhaps
because they were more likely to see leaders in action. For them, as one
alliance member put it, "leadership is the force that makes an organization real."

There is no evidence that GEO and alliance members were looking for
the mythical heroic leader, however. When asked what makes for an effective leader of a high-performing nonprofit, they dismissed the charismatic
leader in favor of a very different model. "They really allow other people
to take part," an alliance member said of the participatory leader. "They
are not controlling. They have controls but they allow freedom for their
staff to do their jobs. If the charismatic founder doesn't change to that
more democratic style, they're gone." A GEO member echoed the
description: "You can't just have a visionary who wants to do it himself

or herself. You have to have a team-builder. You also have to bring people together and entrust others to do the work. You have to help each individual own a piece of the mission. People can be incredibly creative when they are motivated to be part of something bigger than themselves."

Nor did the GEO and alliance members see leadership in the singular. Most talked about leadership as being driven down into the organization through shared values. "It is a real battle for me when people call and ask for leadership training," said one alliance member. "They are looking for an elusive quality that is part charisma, part competency. I see it as people who can get others motivated, a very inclusive quality. It rates at the top because it is so important to everything else, but is very difficult to teach."

Difficult though it may be to teach, graduates of the nation's leading public policy and administration graduate schools say leadership has been essential to their career success. When asked what skills had helped them succeed in their nonprofit jobs, 89 percent of the graduates interviewed by the Center for Public Service in 1998 put maintaining ethical standards first, followed by leading others at 76 percent, and managing conflict at 66 percent.

But when asked to rate how helpful their programs had been in actually teaching those skills, maintaining ethical standards, leading others, and managing conflict were hardly curricular strengths. Eighty-nine percent rated maintaining ethical standards a very important skill, but just 48 percent said their schools had been very helpful in teaching the skill, yielding a 41 percent need-to-help gap; 76 percent rated leading others as very important, but just 39 said their schools had been very helpful in teaching that skill, yielding a 37 percent gap; 66 percent rated managing conflict as very important, but just 23 percent said their schools had been very helpful, yielding a 43 percent gap.[3]

The schools did not do a particularly good job in a final category of nonprofit success: raising money and generating extra revenue. Fifty-one percent of graduates in the nonprofit sector said these skills were very important to their success, compared with just 34 percent of those in the private sector and 19 percent in government. But just 11 percent in the nonprofit sector said their schools had been very helpful in teaching the skill, generating a 40 percent gap.

Whether taught by graduate programs, nonprofit associations, management service organizations, or coaches, a new curriculum on leadership could not be established without more research on just what constitutes high-performance leadership. However, when asked what leaders actually do to build high-performance organizations, the long interviews revealed five central activities:

—*Focus on mission.* Soft as it might sound, two-thirds of the opinion leaders pointed to the importance of building meaning around the organization's mission, including a mix of strategic planning, decisionmaking, and priority-setting skills. "You have to define what your institution is going to be," said an alliance member. "How are you going to differentiate yourself? How do you create your niche? Are there enough customers to go around?" A similar set of questions came from a GEO member: "Being an effective leader has to do with asking what are we doing here, what is important, what is going to lead us to true North? It can't be a solo thing. There is also an element of commitment . . . staying with it for a while . . . hanging in there if it takes a while."

—*Build relationships.* Half of the opinion leaders focused on building relationships both inside and outside the organization, including conflict management with basic outreach skills. "You need somebody who is able to build consensus and create the feeling of ownership, to make clear that everyone has a voice and there is no program with disagreement," said an ARNOVA member. "You also need somebody who can build trust with the community. You can't do that by staying focused on what's happening inside the organization."

—*Motivate people.* Half also focused on motivating people, which included team-building, goal-setting, and communication skills. "I know this is going to sound very wishy-washy," an alliance member said, "but everyone has to know how their piece of the puzzle relates to the mission of the organization. That is the only way that each person can become an effective decisionmaker." A GEO member had a somewhat different answer: "A lot of high functioning organizations have a variety of people who share the leadership role. The key is to motivate the top tier, which motivates the second tier, which motivates the third, and on down. Then, you get the front line to motivate the opposite direction."

—*Manage.* Contrary to the old saying that leaders do the right things, and managers do things right, half of the opinion leaders said the leaders of high-performing organizations must come equipped with basic management skills. "The best thing a leader can do is hire people that they trust," said a GEO member. "In other words, hire people who are qualified and get out of the way. Make sure they know what they are expected to do and leave them alone unless they ask for help." An

ARNOVA member said of his experience in running an organization, "I started out by meeting with every staff member one on one asking what one thing I should fix right away. I'll bet that six or eight of them told me to fix the crabapple tree in the front yard. So about the third or fourth day on the job, we went out and fixed the crabapple tree. It was probably the best decision I ever made."

—*Communicate.* Roughly a third of the opinion leaders mentioned communication, whether in reaching out to external contacts, marketing the organization, or helping the organization focus on mission. "First of all, you need to have a vision," said an alliance member. "What is the desired outcome? How are we going to get there? But the vision is useless unless you can communicate it to other people. I think that people can do miraculous things if they are motivated, one by example, two through words, three through celebrating. Leadership is really the process of creating a sense of connectedness, to the goal, the mission, to the team, whatever it is."

Funders, boards, and executives cannot pursue every characteristic at once, nor are they likely to find any one person with every attribute. Moreover, leadership needs change as the organization moves up the development spiral. They might need one kind of leadership at the very beginning when survival is at stake, and a very different kind of leadership later on, when succession is the issue.

Leadership is so important that some scholars see it as the sole factor in success: "To achieve public purposes, leadership counts. What influences the quality of the education in an elementary school? Leadership by the principal. What determines the quality of life in a prison? Leadership by the warden. What affects the performance of a welfare, training, and employment program? Leadership by the department's top managers."[4]

The question is not at all whether leadership matters, but when and how. That is the central question in the study of innovation, for example, where scholars probably know more about how organizational leaders affect innovation than any other characteristic. Leaders play a central role at virtually every stage of the innovation process, from initiation to implementation, particularly in deploying the resources that carry innovation forward.

At the spark of an idea, leaders cultivate broad organizational support for challenging the status quo, harness the shocks and turbulence that spark the rise of a particular idea. They also control the resources needed to move an idea from sketchbook to final launch. At the developmental stage, leaders provide the continuity as idea people are moved out of the way to make room for implementation specialists. They also manage the changing human emotions involved in bringing an idea to fruition, which some describe as euphoria at the beginning, frustration at development, and a search for closure at the end, together reflecting "some of the most gut-wrenching experiences for innovation participants and managers."[5] Leaders handle the natural mistakes and setbacks encountered along the way and help the organization face the outside world as an idea reaches what might be called "launch velocity."

At the implementation stage, leaders help link the new idea with the old, often by using old stuff in new ways. Leaders also make the critical decision about when to *stop* innovating and offer key interpretations of success and failure. These attributions have an extraordinary impact in shaping the organization's future commitment to innovation, not to mention the careers of key innovation participants.

The leader's work clearly changes over the life of the process, shifting from sponsor to critic, institutional leader to mentor, depending upon the specific stage of the process. Because no single leader can play all four roles equally well, scholars rightly argue that successful innovations demand a mix of leaders, often counterbalanced against each other to protect the organization as a whole: "The innovation sponsor runs interference for the project at corporate levels, while the mentor provides direct supervision, coaching, and counsel to the innovation. The counterbalancing role to this coalition is the critic, who is responsible for reality testing of the innovation against hard-nosed criteria."[6] In turn, the critic must be checked by the institutional leader, whose overall responsibility is to ensure a balance of support and restraint for a given idea. Being what they are, critics will second-guess every new idea to death.

## Looking for Help

This long list of characteristics also leads inevitably to questions about which reforms might make the most difference in creating high-performing nonprofits and where the sector will get the help it needs to improve performance. Bluntly asked, who will help the sector become more nonprofit-like?

Reform fads come and go, of course, which prompted one ARNOVA member to muse about the staying power of the effectiveness movement. "Now the thing that could save it is that people will become sophisticated enough to say that we can't afford to let this be a fad. If it's a fad, you end with people having fairly quick, sometimes overly simplistic notions of what it is and isn't. And it becomes the subject of canned programs and workshops and special technical assistance and initiatives and things like that."

The opinion leaders shared this mixed view of the success of past reforms. As table 3-2 shows, the track record of reform is uneven at best. The opinion leaders saw the greatest gains in performance in the encouragement to do more strategic planning, greater training for executives, increased emphasis on outcomes measures, and the increased openness to using standard business tools. As the table also suggests, the way to get all of the above is to increase funding for capacity-building and management-assistance grants.

Where respondents stood on these reforms depends in part on where they sat. The GEO members were significantly more likely to focus on giving executives more access to training than their peers (51 percent said the intervention had improved performance a great deal compared with just 38 percent and 32 percent of ARNOVA and alliance members, respectively), perhaps because they spend so much time interacting with executives through their work. They were also somewhat less likely to endorse more money for capacity building, perhaps because they know the limits of their budgets.

In turn, ARNOVA and alliance members were much more likely to endorse the importance of management standards (49 percent and 42 percent for the former, respectively, versus just 27 percent for the GEO members), in part because they help design and implement the standards. The ARNOVA members were also more likely than GEO members to endorse collaboration, making nonprofits more visible to the public and encouraging executives to stay a bit longer, whereas alliance and GEO members were significantly less likely to emphasize the importance of external review by the Better Business Bureau, Guidestar, and the National Charities Information Bureau.

There was nearly unanimous opinion, however, on the futility of greater donor involvement or oversight. "Most nonprofits don't want donor involvement," said an ARNOVA member. "They just want the money. Even foundations don't really want donor involvement. When you get donor involvement, you get all these strings that come with it. Or you get a donor who is trying to tell you how to run this, that, or the other. Or you get a donor who only wants to fund this part of your

Table 3-2. *What Has Helped: How Much Have Various Reforms Improved Performance?*[a]

Percent

| Reform | Great deal | Fair | Not too much | Nothing at all |
|---|---|---|---|---|
| Creating management standards | 13 | 39 | 30 | 8 |
| Encouraging nonprofits to collaborate with other nonprofits | 17 | 44 | 30 | 5 |
| Making nonprofits more open to the public and media | 13 | 35 | 39 | 7 |
| Reducing duplication and overlap among nonprofits through mergers and alliances | 12 | 39 | 36 | 6 |
| Strengthening external reviews | 4 | 16 | 48 | 19 |
| Encouraging nonprofits to do more strategic planning | 41 | 46 | 10 | 0 |
| Giving executive directors greater access to training | 40 | 48 | 8 | 0 |
| Encouraging executive directors to stay in their jobs longer | 15 | 35 | 27 | 7 |
| Encouraging more funding for capacity building | 38 | 42 | 14 | 0 |
| Increasing emphasis on the measurement of outcomes | 22 | 44 | 27 | 4 |
| Providing management assistance grants | 28 | 49 | 9 | 1 |
| Increasing openness to using standard business tools | 24 | 53 | 15 | 4 |
| Encouraging more active donor involvement | 8 | 31 | 40 | 14 |

a. N = 250.

agenda, and you spend all your time trying to figure out how to pay for the sewer. The new entrepreneurs want to show you how they became rich and help you run your agency."

The opinion leaders also gave mixed reviews about which organizations are most likely to help improve nonprofit performance. As table 3-3 shows, technical assistance providers were seen as the most helpful, followed by associations of nonprofits, and management service organizations. Government ran dead last, followed by external rating organizations and foundations.

Once again, where respondents stood depended in part on where they sat. Alliance members were the least enthusiastic about foundations as a source of improvement, perhaps because they see the rise in program grants that crowd out funding for capacity building, and the most hopeful

Table 3-3. *Who Will Help: Who Has Helped Improve Nonprofit Sector Performance Most?*[a]

Percent

| Source | Great deal | Fair | Not too much | Nothing at all |
|---|---|---|---|---|
| Foundations | 8 | 34 | 53 | 3 |
| Government | 1 | 13 | 54 | 28 |
| Graduate schools | 16 | 44 | 31 | 3 |
| Management service organizations | 25 | 46 | 20 | 2 |
| External rating organizations | 2 | 16 | 43 | 19 |
| Providers of technical assistance | 30 | 54 | 11 | 2 |
| Associations of nonprofits | 20 | 54 | 21 | 2 |

a. N = 250.

about management support organizations and providers of technical assistance, no doubt in part because that is where they work and who they are. Forty-four percent of alliance members said that providers of technical assistance contribute a great deal to improving nonprofit performance, compared with just 28 percent and 19 percent of GEO and ARNOVA members, respectively.

In turn, ARNOVA members were much more hopeful about both government and graduate schools, the former because they may be more realistic about the level of impact of state and local rules, the latter because that is where many of them work. Twenty-six percent of ARNOVA members said graduate schools contribute a great deal to improvement, compared with just 12 percent and 9 percent of alliance and GEO members, respectively. Asked what capacities matter to organizations, an ARNOVA member called for better training: "To be elliptical about it, it takes a certain amount of understanding to understand what capacity is for your organization. Even having a conceptual framework in which you can understand and think about capacity is, in and of itself, a capacity. It is sort of an intellectual sophistication, a strategic sophistication, and something we try to teach in our master's program."

As they did earlier, GEO members discounted the role of foundations as a source of improvement, perhaps because they see the competition between capacity building and program grants as a zero-sum game in which the former can only be sustained with a reduction in the latter. The GEO members most certainly understood that money matters. "Money does solve a lot of problems," a GEO member said in the long interviews.

"It buys you all the tools, sends your people to seminars, and gives the opportunity to look long term, two-three years out, instead of dealing with the problem of the week or the problem of the day or the problem of the hour." A second GEO member agreed:

> There is very big imbalance in nonprofit organizations. Program is always way ahead of the organizational structures and systems such as human resources, finance, public relations, and anything that nurtures fund-raising—in short, all of the things that nurture and sustain and stabilize the organization itself over the long term. If they have a stable financial base, some of it earned, nonprofits have much more freedom to do creative things with their programs. But if they are dependent on program grants for every last cent, they can run themselves into the ground.

Not surprisingly, the three groups vary greatly on who should actually supply the capacity. Alliance members who participated in the long interviews tended to like consultants. "It is very difficult for staff to assess themselves well," said an alliance member. "A strong board could do it without a consultant, but most of the organizations I'm involved with don't have a strong board. In almost all cases, they have to have an outside technical assistance provider."

Alliance members were not the only respondents in love with consultants, however. "The foundation world has just fallen in love with management consultants," a GEO member noted. "They just love them. And, by the way, I do, too. These are folks who will tell you in a very convincing way that it is possible to do a much better job."

Most of the GEO members preferred to use management support organizations. "When you broker with a local service organization," said one grantmaker, "you're dealing with a full service shop. Most do at least some research on the local area, and provide some of the leadership that you would expect from a community foundation. We also like intermediaries. The funders already have enough influence as it is. They already have a big stick."

Another grantmaker explained the role of intermediaries as "a little bit of a smoke screen. We got very deep into capacity building with a number of organizations over the years. In the beginning, they didn't have any reason to trust us. So we used a local management association. We were trying to reduce our profile, reduce our power, because we wanted them to trust us, but didn't want them to be fooled about who was writing the checks."

## The One True Thing?

Before turning to what the executives of the 250 high-performing nonprofits actually said about their own organizations, it is important to look at the answers to one last question from the survey of opinion leaders. When given an open-ended opportunity to offer one piece of advice for improving the performance of nonprofits, the opinion leaders rejected one true thing for a mixed list of investments: (1) a mix of recruiting, paying, and developing talented staff, boards, and volunteers (19 percent); (2) planning and clarifying mission (18 percent); (3) funding for operations and capacity building (16 percent); (4) collaborating outside the organization with other nonprofits and inside the organization through better staff/board relationships (10 percent); (5) pure technical assistance (4 percent); (6) new technology (2 percent); and (7) more research (1.6 percent).

As with any such open-ended question, several responses were nearly impossible to categorize, including the suggestion that the sector get rid of the term "nonprofit" as "a license to be fiscally irresponsible" and the recommendation that the sector adopt a "dialectical organizational model" with "inspiring leaders, values driven, flat organizations, with upward flow of information, and participatory leadership." Perhaps the best advice of all, therefore, came from the two respondents who said, "Do away with the one-size-fits-all mentality" and "You can't do any one thing in isolation—capacity building has to be holistic." Simply stated, the one true thing about achieving and sustaining high performance is that there is no one true thing.

## Conclusion

Like the Minnesota and Maryland standards, the opinion leaders tend to see high performers as practically perfect in every way. Buried in the all their advice are three simple messages of aspiration. First, the opinion leaders believe that high performance is possible, if not always prevalent. The nonprofit sector hardly needs to look over the walls into the private sector or government for examples of ordinary excellence. After all, there were almost 500 nonprofits that made their list of exemplars.

Second, the opinion leaders also agreed that there is a very simple place to start the journey toward high performance. Leadership does appear to be the answer, but not the kind of sparkly, charismatic leadership celebrated in glossy best-sellers, or the aggressive, chainsaw, Attila-the-Hun leadership recounted in corporate boardrooms. Rather, it is a participatory, democratic leadership that draws upon strengths inside and outside the organization. To leaders who think they must go it alone, the opinion leaders say otherwise.

Third, there is no single pathway to improving performance. Some of the high performers no doubt started with strategic planning, others with training, still others with a new financial management system. But they all got started. Nonprofits that are waiting for someone to discover the one best way to high performance might as well be waiting for Godot.

This is not to argue that every last insight from the opinion leaders will hold in the real world. As chapter 4 shows, the exemplars have a somewhat narrower list of suggestions for starting the journey toward high performance. In a single word, they say start with the sector's greatest asset, people.

## CHAPTER FOUR

# Views from the Front Lines

Being business-like may be a major concern for theorists, grantmakers, and think-tank scholars, but not for executives. Much as they worry about competition from private firms, the new role of venture philanthropy, and the corporate pressure on their boards, most of the executives interviewed for this report are ready to do whatever it takes to succeed. If that means importing ideas from the private sector, so be it.

The barrier to achieving and sustaining higher performance is not a lack of ideas, however. The tides of nonprofit reform produce plenty of ideas for any executive director or board willing to look. Rather, the greatest challenge appears to be rooted in the notion that nonprofit-like means doing more with less under unyielding pressure. "We are expected to run on a shoestring," said the head of a food distribution program. "We are expected to do with less than a for-profit as far as equipment or desks or anything else that comes down the pike. We have this second-hand, make-do attitude. That's a hard thing for me to say, but I think we accept less than the best."[1]

A youth service executive agreed: "We are caught in this really weird position where we are getting our money from people who are twice removed from the people we serve. It's very difficult to figure out how to stay true to your mission, how to listen to the people you serve, and still get the money from the people who are so many steps away. Give all the people we serve the money so they can buy what we do, and we'll run our organization like a for-profit. You want efficiency? That's how you get efficiency."

Not all executives equated nonprofit-like with second-class status. As one dropout prevention program director argued, "I'd like to see anybody operate with the restrictions that we face on how we do business. That little bit of mythology is going to change over the next few years as the for-profit world starts seeing that they can learn from the way we do business." An environmental advocacy executive made a similar point: "If we were in the business of making widgets, I would have been a millionaire long ago and would have retired by now. The profits would have been just astounding, just because the work we do is always more than anyone could have expected from our resource base."

Yet much as they talked about the ability to do more with less, many of the executives worried about balancing the pressure for improvement against the reality of uncertain funding streams and rising public expectations. In the long interviews that followed the structured telephone survey, over half of the twenty-five executives stated that the greatest challenges of the future would be to raise sufficient funds for both infrastructure and mission.

Asked what challenges she faced in improving her organization's performance, the executive director of a youth organization answered with four words: "Bringing in enough money. We get program funding for things that we're already doing, but we need money that is not tied to anything. We made a decision some time ago to stop going after insignificant one-year grants, particularly ones that require you to set up a whole program and operate it for a year. We are actually working on raising what we're calling leap-year funding where we're going to raise twice as much in one year than we need. Wouldn't that be wonderful?"

Before exploring these and other opinions about high performance, it is important to ask whether the sample of 250 high-performing organizations is actually composed of high-performing organizations. Are they true high performers or just highly visible? Are they actually producing results or merely producing reputations? The answer is both "yes" and "yes."

On the one hand, if being a high-performing organization involves networking, communicating, and fund-raising, high performers are more likely to be known to grantmakers, scholars, and technical assistance providers than organizations that do not advertise themselves.

High performers are highly visible in part because that is a feature of high performance. On the other hand, high performance cannot simply reside in reputation. Good as they are at communicating, high performers must also be good at producing program impacts. Although they do not have to be practically perfect in every way, they must be effective in their work.

When asked why they thought they had been nominated for the study, almost half of the twenty-five organizations interviewed in depth pointed to their teamwork and quality of staff, just over a third emphasized their programmatic impact, a quarter focused on their mission, and another quarter on their effectiveness. "We do what we say we're going to do," one director of a food center responded. "We don't stray from our mission, we fully report all of our product, our finances are open to the public, and our credibility is on view for the entire city to see."

Others echoed this blend of programmatic impact and managerial integrity. "Because we achieve things you can feel and measure and see," said the director of an environmental advocacy group. "Because we deliver surprising results," said the head of children's group. "I know that we have a very clear sense of what we're here for," said the executive director of a religious education center. "Because we have a very high-quality staff and have very low turnover, and we meet or exceed our goals," said a school outreach program director. "Because everybody who works at the organization and serves on the board is completely aligned with the council's mission and role," said the head of a northeastern environmental advocacy agency. "There is no mistaking who we are and what we are prepared to do in defense of the environment." A community development executive summed the themes up as follows: "Our mission is fairly distilled and is what we measure against, and we try to integrate those values into our outcome measures. I think we are effective because we have diversified our funding sources pretty broadly. We have roughly 1,400 different sources of funding, including our individual givers, and that enables us to have some integrity in the way we do things. From a management perspective, we have strong people coming here even though there are a lot of opportunities to make more money in other places."

Altogether, these organizations were remarkably modest about their accomplishments, even though several are national award winners. If these twenty-five made the list because of boasting or overselling, it is not evident in the transcripts of their interviews. Although they were certainly willing to talk about what they did well, they understood that high performance involves a never-ending journey and continuous improvement.

## Talking about Effectiveness Again

The 250 executives serve as a check on the description of the practically perfect nonprofit offered by the 250 members of GEO, ARNOVA, and the Alliance for Nonprofit Management, bringing the portrait into much sharper focus. The search is for matches between what the opinion leaders saw more generally and what their own nominees saw specifically. To the extent that the two surveys match, one can argue that a given characteristic is a true state of preferred organizational being. To the extent that the two surveys diverge, one can argue that the opinion leaders may have overstated the importance of a characteristic.

Even a cursory side-by-side review of the two surveys suggests one simple finding. As mentioned earlier, there is no one best pathway to higher performance. There are high-performing nonprofits for just about every taste: large and small, specialized and generalist, and national and local. And there are high performers in virtually every possible corner of the nonprofit sector: 6 percent of the 250 in the sample focused on arts and culture, 4 percent on the environment, 8 percent on community development, 12 percent on housing, 11 percent on children and youth, and 7 percent on health. The rest were spread across a host of other specialties.

### Defining Terms

The opinion leaders and executives shared a similar understanding of organizational effectiveness. Like the opinion leaders, the executives put mission at the center of the term. "All the components are in place that will enable you to go forward with your mission." "Being able to have the desired impact." "Doing what we preach." "Demonstrable results." "Using resources to get the greatest impact." "That you achieve a little more than you set out to do." "It means we are providing effective services that are outcomes driven, that we manage our money well, hold public trust high, put the focus on issues of performance and developing appropriate services." Although several executives dismissed the term as being just another buzzword, half used the word "mission" somewhere in their answer, and two-thirds equated effectiveness with being focused on achieving measurable results.

## Table 4-1. *Disagreeing with Contradictions*[a]

| An organization can be very effective in achieving its program goals but not be well managed | An organization can be very well managed and still not achieve its program goals | | | |
| --- | --- | --- | --- | --- |
| | Strongly agree and somewhat agree | | Somewhat disagree and strongly disagree | |
| | Opinion leaders | Executives | Opinion leaders | Executives |
| Strongly agree and somewhat agree | 57 | 39 | 23 | 37 |
| Somewhat disagree and strongly disagree | 11 | 9 | 10 | 15 |

a. N = 247 for opinion leaders, 250 for executive directors. Each cell shows the percentage of all respondents.

Whatever the specific definition, these executives agreed on the role of management as a necessary condition of impacts. Whereas 44 percent of the opinion leaders strongly agreed that an organization can be very well managed and still not achieve its program goals, only 35 percent of the executives agreed. More significantly, whereas 27 percent of the opinion leaders strongly agreed that an organization can be very effective in achieving its program goals and still not be well managed, only 16 percent of the executives agreed.

The importance of management to the executives is particularly clear when the two questions are combined in table 4-1. The executives were significantly less likely to believe that organizations could have their cake and eat it, too, meaning be very effective and not well managed. Whereas 57 percent of the opinion leaders agreed that an organization could be both (a) very effective in achieving its program goals and not well managed, and (b) very well managed and still not achieve its program goals, only 39 percent of the executives agreed with both statements. In short, executives were significantly less likely to believe that an organization could be very effective in achieving its program goals and not be well managed.

This focus on being well managed carried into the questions about the words that best describe a high-performing organization. When asked which one word is the most important characteristic of a high-performing nonprofit organization, the executive directors put the words in the following order: (1) innovative (26 percent), (2) principled (23 percent),

(3) entrepreneurial (19 percent), (4) collaborative (18 percent), (5) resilient (10 percent), and (6) rigorous (4 percent).

Interestingly, the opinion leaders offered a very different order when asked how well each word described high-performing organizations. Recall that 76 percent of opinion leaders said the word "principled" described high performers very well, compared with 72 percent who said the same of "resilient," 64 percent who said "innovative," 51 percent who said "collaborative," 40 percent who said "rigorous," and just 37 percent who said "entrepreneurial."

The question is how "resilient" could be so high and "entrepreneurial" so low on the opinion leaders' list, but in almost exactly the reverse order among the executives. One answer may be the wording of the question. The executives were asked to pick the most important word for describing high performance, while the opinion leaders were allowed to rate each word separately, which may have allowed "resilient" to rise higher than it otherwise would have.

The wording of questions is a less compelling explanation for the relative rankings of the word "entrepreneurial." At least for the executives, there appear to be two mental models of what it means to be a high-performing nonprofit, one built around the words "innovative" and "entrepreneurial," and the other centered on "principled" and "collaborative." Executives who put the emphasis on innovative and entrepreneurial pathways did operate somewhat different organizations from executives who focused on principled and collaborative methods.

Although some readers might be tempted to juxtapose the two models as "for-profit" versus "nonprofit," the two groups of executives were more alike than different on most opinions. Both were equally likely to have spent all or most of their career in the nonprofit sector, be the founding director of their organizations, believe that high-performing nonprofits need leaders who know how to motivate people, agree that organizations can be very well managed and still not achieve their program goals, and say their organizations collaborate with other nonprofits.

This is not to deny the differences between the two. Executives who emphasized entrepreneurial and innovative values lead organizations that raise more self-generated revenue, put a heavier emphasis on fund-raising, and have a more diversified funding base than executives who picked principled and collaborative. The data suggest that these are, in fact, two slightly different approaches to designing nonprofit organizations: one is a more opportunistic, revenue-generating approach (entrepreneurial + innovative), and the other a more deliberative, consensus-building approach (principled + collaborative). Each one has its advantages and disadvantages as a pathway to higher performance.

### The Pressure to Improve

Whatever pathway they took, the executives certainly felt the pressure to become more effective. Not all felt it emanating from the same place, however. Some executives felt the pressure from outside their organizations, whether from funders, government, or a more generalized demand for high performance. "Funders have suddenly realized that billions of dollars are going into the sector and we still have social problems in this country," the executive director of a volunteer service noted. "Somehow, they want to know what happened. "We gave all this money out there and nothing seems to have changed substantially." The head of a religious education agency agreed: "I know the foundations we deal with wouldn't give us a nickel if we didn't produce good graphs that show we know what we're doing. And they've actually gotten more competitive during the years I've been here. There's a whole lot less tolerance in the community for poorly performing nonprofits. People's time today is much more valuable than it was—and that goes for funders, staff, and volunteers."

The executive director of a youth service organization pointed more broadly to the general trend coming from government and communities. "We're seeing it from funders, we're seeing it from the public sector. This actually coincides with the 'smart government' movement that is trying to develop indicators for public sector performance. So this isn't happening in a vacuum." This executive also pointed to the growth in the sector as a source of pressure:

> The sector has almost reached a critical mass where it naturally forces society to ask tougher questions. I think that's true not just in this country, but globally with the rise of NGOs [nongovernmental organizations]. There are just some fundamental tensions that arise with growth—tensions of control, tensions of accountability and scale based on the ability of these organizations to greatly affect communities through their work. That's a natural progression tied to the growth of the sector.

Despite this sense of outside pressure, many of the executives expressed an internal commitment to organizational effectiveness. "I predict in a few years that nobody will say that this is funder driven," said the executive director of a dropout prevention program. "At that point, it will become so institutionalized that it's just the way you do business. No one will question it." The executive director of an opera company already felt that internal pressure. "The pressures are on us to do better, and keep our place in a market that is constantly changing. We are not reacting to anybody from the outside telling us to improve. What we are doing is getting the data and asking what it says to us." As the head of a rehabilitation center noted, "I don't know that anybody has applied a pressure to us to be more effective. It's just an ongoing process of looking at what we're doing and how we're doing it. Are there needs of our patients that we haven't been meeting? Are there new opportunities? We are applying that pressure to ourselves and, therefore, it's not coming from the outside."

## The Demographics of High Performance

All nonprofits may not be equal in size, age, and purpose, but the actual demographics of the 250 high-performing nonprofits surveyed for this report suggest that improvement is possible under both the best and worst of circumstances. Small, young, virtually unknown nonprofits showed up in the sample, as did large, older, highly visible nonprofits such as the Nature Conservancy, Habitat for Humanity, CARE, and the national Red Cross.

The presence of the Red Cross in this sample is particularly instructive for those who might argue that high performance is easily maintained by national exemplars. The fact is that achieving high performance is only part of the challenge facing the nonprofit sector. As the Red Cross case suggests, sustaining high performance through continuous investment and improvement is also essential.

Size and reputation are both a blessing and a curse for large organizations such as the Red Cross. Even as they attract millions in restricted funding for everything from disaster relief to land acquisition, these organizations are often unable to amass the needed capital needed for long-term effectiveness. Donors want their money to go directly to program impacts, even if that means neglecting to address the fact that large organizations cannot communicate with their field offices, purchase new refrigerators, or maintain the land they acquire.

Moreover, some of these systems are so expensive that no single national foundation could provide the necessary funding even if it dedicated itself entirely to the task. As a result, large organizations often make needed investments on an ad hoc basis, adding pieces of new systems year after year until they can finally complete the task. Not unlike government agencies such as the Federal Aviation Administration and Internal Revenue Service, these organizations find that this piecemeal approach guarantees they will always be generations behind the leading edge.

The problems of size may help explain the demographics of the sample of 250 high performers studied here. The majority of the high performers are neither very large nor very small, and most are certainly not very young. Only 12 percent had budgets under $500,000, only 25 percent had fewer than fifteen employees, only 26 percent had fewer than thirty volunteers, and only 8 percent were younger than seven. Although there were very large, old, national organizations in the sample, the bulk of the high performers were in between large and small.

## How Size Matters

Size was by far the most significant predictor of how these organizations structured themselves. It was also highly related to age. Not surprisingly, younger organizations were more likely to be smaller. More than half of the nonprofits running at or less than $1 million a year were fifteen years old or younger, compared with 19 percent of organizations running at $2 million to $10 million, and just 7 percent of organizations running at more than $10 million. Conversely, 79 percent of the large organizations were more than thirty years old, compared with 42 percent of the medium-size organizations, and just 18 percent of the small organizations.

Age and size are related in other ways. Seventy-seven percent of organizations with more than 100 employees were over thirty years old, compared with just 4 percent of organizations under seven years old. And 50 percent of organizations with more than 100 volunteers were more than thirty years old, compared with just 5 percent of organizations under seven years old.

The question is whether age or budget is the driver for these patterns. Are older organizations more likely to be big, or vice versa? It is nearly impossible to untangle the relationship in this sample of high performers.

Whereas 16 of the 105 organizations over thirty years old operated at $1 million or less, just one of the 20 organizations under the age of seven operated at more than $10 million.

What is clear is that size matters to what high-performing organizations do. In dealing with the external environment, smaller nonprofits (defined as operating at under $1 million a year) were much more likely than the largest (defined as operating at more than $10 million) to rely on volunteers to deliver at least some of their services, while larger organizations were more likely to regularly survey their clients regarding programs and services, a pattern that makes perfect sense. Money buys employees and surveys. (These patterns can be reviewed in appendix B, which presents the executive director data by size.)

In dealing with their internal structures, smaller organizations were likely to have many fewer layers of management and say that staff from different parts of the organization work together than larger, while larger ones were more likely to have diverse staffs, reserve funds, and difficulty recruiting staff, but not boards. Asked about layers of management, for example, more than two-thirds of the small organizations had zero, one, or two layers, compared with just a sixth of their larger peers.

Again, the pattern makes perfect sense. Size begets formalization, which begets rules and red tape. At the same time, size produces dollars. Only 10 percent of smaller organizations said they had a large reserve fund, compared with 40 percent of larger organizations. Smaller organizations were also slightly less likely to use information technology such as e-mail and the Internet to enhance performance.

On leadership, executives at smaller organizations reported difficulty with their boards on all fronts, from having clear understandings of board responsibilities to setting policy and overseeing the organization's performance. Barely half of the small organizations said their boards were clear on general responsibilities, compared with three-quarters of the large nonprofits.

Size helps with board development on several levels. It most certainly provides the funding for board development and may help attract a more engaged board and executives who have the skills to clarify board/staff relationships. However, size does not produce more board activity. It was the small high performer that met with its board much more frequently than the large one: 41 percent of the small organizations met with their boards at least nine times a year, compared with just 26 percent of the largest organizations.

Size also shapes impressions of the kind of leadership needed for high performance. Although size made no difference in the characteristics executives found important in a high-performing nonprofit, the executives of small organizations were more likely to believe a charismatic leader important, while those at larger organizations were more likely to emphasize having a decisive leader. And when forced to choose the most important leadership characteristic of a high-performer nonprofit, 56 percent of the executives at the largest organizations picked "honest," compared with just 37 percent of the executives at the smaller organizations.

In dealing with their internal structures, large organizations have obvious advantages over small ones in linking staff pay to performance, creating position descriptions, and investing resources in staff training. Once again, size produces more resources coupled with greater formalization. What it does not produce is any greater desire to measure outcomes or use data to make decisions, or any greater likelihood of having a fast, accurate accounting system. Large and small high performers are equally committed to all three goals.

## Size and Improvement

Size also made a difference to recommendations for improvement. Asked what they would recommend to another similar nonprofit on how to become a high-performing organization, 60 percent of the executives at the small organizations recommended first working on becoming well managed, compared with 48 percent of the executives at larger organizations. In turn, 45 percent of the executives at larger organizations emphasized increasing program impacts first, compared with 26 percent of the executives at the smaller organizations. One suspects the pattern reflects the reality that larger organizations already have met a basic test on management, whereas smaller are still struggling to strengthen management.

Asked how important it is for below-average performers to focus on improving the four areas of organizational life, 62 percent of the executives at the smaller organizations said that improving external relationships was very important, compared with 55 percent of the executives at the larger organizations, while 88 percent of the executives at the larger organizations said it was very important to improve internal management systems, compared with 74 percent of the executives at the smaller nonprofits.

Asked to choose which area a below-average organization should improve first, the executives at smaller organizations were significantly more likely to instruct their peers to start with internal structure, while the executives at larger organizations were more likely to emphasize leadership. Whereas 22 percent of the small-organization executives said first work on internal structure, only 2 percent of the largest-organization executives agreed, and whereas 83 percent of the big-organization directors said first work on leadership, only 53 percent of the small-organization executives agreed.

Finally, size mattered to perceptions of reform and reformers. Executives at small organizations had less confidence in graduate schools that train nonprofit executives and staff or in management service organizations, and more confidence in associations of nonprofits than their peers at big organizations. In turn, executives at large organizations placed more hope in management standards and outcome measures, whereas executives at small organizations put more faith in management assistance grants.

These differences by size (and by implication, age) offer at least some direction to the organizational effectiveness movement on capacity-building interventions. Smaller, younger organizations show a greater need for interventions that focus on generating revenue, measuring outcomes, strengthening basic organizational design, exploiting e-mail and other information technologies, and developing a board. In contrast, larger organizations may need little help in the area of internal mechanics, but a great deal in organizational reform, delayering, and liberation from the rules they have developed over the years.

These differences by size should not obscure the substantial agreement among the high performers on many of the characteristics discussed next. There were many more agreements on how to design high performers than disagreements. Large or small, young or old, all of these high performers agreed on the need to improve.

—None disagreed on the need to collaborate in external relationships, or, one suspects, on the need for access to at least some unrestricted revenue.

—None disagreed on the need to give staff the freedom to make decisions in order to improve internal structure, or, one suspects again, on the need to increase staff diversity, reduce the layers between the top and bottom, or build a rainy-day fund.

—None disagreed that the leadership should encourage staff to take risks and try new things, that communication among staff and management should flow freely, or that the board must know its job.

Table 4-2. *Demographics of Executive Directors*[a]

Percent

| Characteristic | Total | Small (< $1 million) | Medium ($2 million to $10 million) | Large (> $10 million) |
|---|---|---|---|---|
| Male | 45 | 39 | 42 | 62 |
| White | 87 | 84 | 90 | 84 |
| < 40 years of age | 15 | 27 | 8 | 7 |
| > 50 years of age | 58 | 47 | 60 | 71 |
| Founding director still running the organization | 41 | 49 | 31 | 42 |

a. N = 250.

—None disagreed on the internal importance of accurate accounting systems or strategic planning, or of more resources for training and implementing an effective pay-for-performance system.

Size may have played its most important role in shaping the demographics of the 250 executives. As table 4-2 shows, women and younger executives were much more likely to be found at smaller organizations, men and older executives were more likely to be found at larger organizations, and race was more evenly distributed across all sizes of organization.

The data reveal not only a glass ceiling at larger nonprofits but a significant age bulge moving through the sector. About half of the executives interviewed for this report will be eligible for retirement by 2010, prompting serious questions about whether the sector is ready for the coming leadership transition. Whatever their age and size, few nonprofits have succession plans, and even fewer funders provide grants for succession planning. As a result, the sector is woefully unprepared for the shock it will face as an entire generation of baby boom executives leaves over the next decade.

Contrary to the views of the opinion leaders, the data also suggest that high performance is quite possible under founding directors. Although the percentages of founding and nonfounding directors are roughly equal at small and large organizations, founding directors are much less likely to be in charge of midsize organizations. This suggests that many small organizations must jettison their founder in order to move to the next size level. If founding directors can survive this awkward middle size, they do very well at surviving for the long term.

Because age and size of organizations are so highly correlated, it is no surprise that women, younger executives, and executives of color would be found at young organizations (fifteen years old or younger), and not at older organizations (more than thirty years old). Indeed, 69 percent of young organizations are headed by women, compared with just 45 percent of older organizations; 35 percent of young executives (under forty years of age) are at young organizations, compared with just 5 percent at older organizations; and 20 percent of the executives at young organizations are nonwhite, compared with just 13 percent at older organizations. To the extent that the nonprofit sector sharply constrains the number of new organizations in coming years, it will lose an important training ground for the young, female, and nonwhite executives it needs to fill the leadership posts about to be vacated by the older, male, and white executives at its larger, flagship organizations.

## Actual State of Being Nonprofit-like

Although considered practically perfect by the opinion leaders who nominated them, the 250 high-performing organizations were far from perfect. As the long interviews suggest, many struggle with basic management challenges such as recruiting good staff, managing board/staff relationships, raising enough money to keep up with technology, and avoiding dependency on any revenue source. Much as they may dream of becoming the practically perfect nonprofit, many of the high performers must deal with the ordinary frustrations that arise in all human organizations. "My only reward is seeing the program succeed," said an executive of a Colorado religious education agency. "And in order to see it succeed, we have to bounce off a lot of rocks in the river. There isn't a day that goes by when there aren't challenges to test the organization. As we're bumping around on those rocks, I've got to remind myself that the vision is strong, the mission is clear, and God's going to take care of us if we just keep doing what's in front of us."

Many high performers often hit those rocks under extraordinary pressure to grow. "We are building the plane while we're flying it," one executive director remarked. Another mused about the challenges he faced because of the "skills I don't have, the time I don't have, the other dreams that are on the drawing board that are going to stop me from getting to something that, in hindsight, may turn out to be more important. If somebody asked me how confident I felt that I've positioned the organization right for the next three to four years, I'd say, 'Wow, I think I've got it right.' But if somebody asked about the next ten years, I can't say what is going to happen."

The challenge for most of these executives is not raising more money. There is nothing funders like to do more, it seems, than give more funding to high-performing organizations. Rather, the major challenge is balancing the short term against the long term. "If somebody wrote me a check tomorrow for a million dollars, that would solve my short-term needs," said the executive director of a religious education organization. "But it wouldn't solve any long-term needs for this agency. We've got to continue to spread the vision of what we do, continue to bring on staff and lay leaders who have that passion burning inside. We have to bring it to the surface so they will become ambassadors and advocates for our mission. Then the funds will come."

Hard as it is to resolve this tension in a high-performing organization, it is infinitely more difficult in organizations that are just beginning the journey to higher performance. Should they buy a new telephone system or develop a strategic plan? Should they put their money into health care benefits for their staffs or into computers? Should they hire a fund-raiser or a coach? The high performers interviewed for this report would likely answer "all of the above." They are not high performers for nothing.

But the high performers would almost certainly ask the poorly performing organization where it wants to go. Why begin the journey if getting there will make no difference? As such, the journey toward higher performance is driven inexorably forward by the knowledge that it is a journey worth taking.

In a sense, organizations that do not know why they exist and who they serve will never make the right choices, while those that frame each question with a clear sense of mission will almost never make the wrong choices. "It starts with focus, focus, focus," said the director of an environmental organization. "Too many advocacy organizations run around attempting to put out fires. They seldom, if ever, get at the cause of the fires." "I think about it multiple times every day," said the director of a nonprofit technical assistance agency. "It's a filter through which I make every decision. It just always has been there. Every single day I'm stunned at the small decisions and the large decisions where you either take a step forward in pursuing your mission or not."

Even acknowledging the hundreds of small and large choices along the way, it is also important to note that high performers do share common characteristics that can be called preferred states of organizational being. As the following pages suggest, the sequencing of change may be different for every organization, but the ultimate destination looks remarkably similar. Unfortunately, there were not enough nonprofits in the study to draw conclusions about differences between types of nonprofits by subject area such as arts, environment, homelessness, and so forth.[2]

## External Relationships

The 250 high-performing nonprofits mostly take the outside world as a given. Although they do work hard to increase their market presence through fund-raising, collaboration, and efforts to generate revenues, they appear to believe that they can only do so much as individual organizations to change the world around them.

The problem is that the outside world is changing with or without them. "Many of our current subscribers, donors, and single-ticket buyers will die in the next decade—those who are now in their sixties and seventies," said an opera director. "And they are not going to be as readily replaced as they were for the last twenty years because the tree from which they can be picked does not have as much ripe fruit on it."

So what does an organization that features operas composed by dead Europeans do to cultivate a new audience in a city in which whites are already in the minority? For starters, this opera company is trying to increase awareness of opera as a life-enriching experience for all citizens:

> That is why we have a vigorous education program that works very seriously in so-called underserved areas to create awareness for a new generation of audiences. That is why we have "super titles" so people can understand the words in *Traviata*. I was one of the people who objected to super titles when they were first talked about back in the early 1980s. I said that is nonsense, what a terrible thing. Then I saw a performance of *Traviata* with titles for school kids. And I watched children crying in the opera at the right moments. I saw teenage girls everywhere bursting into tears. I came back to my board and said I have been a fool, we are going to do

titles. And that is why we will probably put in large television screens for the cheap seats. I am not really in favor of the screens, but I am also coldly practical. Titles are where we are going, and screens are where we are going. And I will just cry the first time we use the screens, and then everybody will say, "Gee, what a great idea." And I will say I knew it always was.

In addition, the opera is an active advocate on behalf of the arts: "If you look at our staff of forty, I would guess that at least twenty of us serve on community boards. This is the staff, mind you, not our board, but the paid staff. I am on the board of the Convention and Visitors Bureau, not because a lot of audience is visitors, but because conventions and visitors are vital to the operations of our city. . . . That has got nothing to do with the opera company. It has to do with the growth of the city."

Asked what he would recommend to other organizations by way of shaping the environment, this executive offered a remarkably simple suggestion:

> I urge my colleagues in the world of opera to join the local Rotary Club, get only to the major business committees in tow. You only win by doing that, because these people who think the arts are airy-fairy stuff realize that you are their equal, that you are worthy of their respect. And, therefore, so is your institution. They know that if they give us a dollar it is not wasted. So we win in that regard. But I have also found that the more I am involved in the community, the more I love this city, and the more I care about what happens. And if you involve yourself in the community, the arts can make a difference in the community on many more levels than purely artistic.

This opera company is hardly alone among the high performers in engaging its community. It is safe to say that all of the high-performing nonprofits work hard to be known within their communities, whether by joining boards, committees, and associations, or through the Internet, newsletters, and other advertising. In their other external relationships, the 250 high performers behave almost exactly as the opinion leaders described them, sharing five basic approaches to the outside world. Recall that a characteristic is considered shared if more than half of the executives said it existed in their organizations.

—*Collaborate*. Seventy-five percent of the executives said their organizations collaborate with other organizations to a large extent, with no statistically significant differences between small, medium, or large organizations. Both the opinion leaders and the executives rated "collaborate" first.

—*Measure*. Sixty-four percent of the executives said their organizations measure the results or outcomes of what they do, with large organizations the most likely to say they measure to a large extent. Three-quarters of the high performers with annual budgets over $10 million say they measure, compared with three-fifths of the medium and small organizations, probably because size generates the revenues, pressures, and professionalization needed to build the internal capacity to measure. The opinion leaders rated measurement fifth.

—*Diversify*. Fifty-six percent of the 250 high performers said they have a diversified funding base. The larger the organization, however, the greater the diversity. It is entirely possible that organizations only get larger through diversification, which would mean that this characteristic is less a cause of high performance than a consequence. The opinion leaders also rated diversified funding third.

—*Know the client*. Fifty-four percent of the high performers said they regularly survey their clients regarding programs and services. Once again, however, the larger organizations were the most likely to report this characteristic, again no doubt in part because size generates the resources needed to conduct surveys. Recall that only 41 percent of the opinion leaders saw surveying among most of the high performers they knew.

—*Make money*. Fifty-three percent of the high performers said that they generate at least some unrestricted revenues. As with diversification, larger organizations are more likely to say this characteristic describes them to a large extent, again in part because the ability to generate revenue is one possible explanation for their size. The opinion leaders rated making money second.

As predicted by the opinion leaders, virtually all of the high performers said they had experienced significant growth in the demand for their programs and services over the past five years. Interestingly, 86 percent of small nonprofits said they had experienced a large amount of growth, followed by medium-size nonprofits at 76 percent, and large organizations at 72 percent. That might help explain the underinvestment in diversification, measurement, surveys, and revenue generation. Simply put, smaller organizations may be growing so fast that they cannot bother with measurement and surveys, may have little time for diversification, and may not need to generate revenue.

Like the opinion leaders, these executive directors did not see the outside world as a particularly hostile place. Twenty-seven percent said the word "competitive" described the external environment very well, followed by "heavily regulated" at 15 percent, and "turbulent" at just 12 percent. However, larger organizations were significantly more likely than smaller ones to see the external environment as competitive, regulated, and turbulent, perhaps because smaller organizations can find and hold a niche more easily or constitute less of a target for other organizations.

As noted earlier, all of these organizations interact with their environment at some level, if only to generate grants and contracts. But many also market their organizations aggressively. "If you are a leader in the nonprofit sector," said the head of a volunteer placement agency, "you really have to know your mission. But then you need to have a strong marketing plan that has as many elements as possible so you are consistently getting the word out about who you are, who you serve, or what service you provide. Whether you are a symphony or a hospital, you have to generate public awareness, both to get clients and to raise money."

Even as she talked about marketing, this executive director also emphasized the need for relationship building. "You don't have to have lunch and breakfast with everybody, but you do need to be out there meeting political people, elected officials, funders, and key decisionmakers in the community and media. All of these people play a role in your success and need to know of your existence." The director of a homeless center confirmed the importance of building relationships: "We spend a tremendous amount of time, energy, and resources in developing what I call community capacity—the capacity of this community to care for the most marginalized of this community. That involves the development of relationships, partnerships, and services to help the people we serve develop their own capacity to take back ownership of their lives."

Despite their commitment to building relationships, few of these high performers appear to engage in political advocacy on behalf of their own organizations or their communities as a whole. They may meet with political leaders and interact with the news media, but most of these high performers would never lobby the state legislature, file a lawsuit, or protest budget cutbacks. Like most nonprofits in general, they tend to focus only on the outside world that affects them directly, meaning the grantmakers, donors, and government agencies that control their revenues. Unless advocacy is in their charter, the outside world is taken as a given, in part because so many nonprofits mistakenly believe that they are prohibited from anything else.

## Internal Structure

Bureaucracy may be an unfamiliar term in the nonprofit sector, but there are certainly organizations that might be called bureaucratic among the 250 high performers surveyed for this report. As already mentioned, the larger the organization, the more formal the hierarchy. Over half of the largest high performers had at least four layers between the top and bottom of the organization, compared with just 1 percent of the smallest high performers.

Regardless of size, the high performers have at least seven structural characteristics in common:

—*Push authority downward.* No matter how dense their hierarchies, 79 percent of the executives said that staff make routine decisions on their own. Interestingly, smaller organizations were slightly more likely to ask staff to consult with the executive or senior staff when making routine decisions, perhaps because they are small enough or flat enough to allow such easy interaction. Opinion leaders rated this characteristic second.

—*Exploit technology.* Eighty percent of the high performers said their organizations use information technology such as e-mail and the Internet to enhance performance. As expected given their budgets, smaller organizations were slightly less likely to exploit technology effectively. When asked later in the survey to describe their technological infrastructure, however, less than half of the executives said their technology was very adequate, suggesting that many of the high performers use e-mail and the Internet to the best of their ability, not to the best of technology. Opinion leaders rated this characteristic first.

—*Work in teams and collaborate internally.* Eighty-two percent of the executives said their organizations encourage their staffs to work in teams, and nearly as many strongly disagreed that staff from different parts of their organizations rarely work together. However, much as larger organizations subscribed to the general ideal of teamwork, they were significantly less likely than small organizations to say that staff from different parts of the organization work together. Larger organizations may want their staff to work in teams, but they must work harder to breach the bureaucratic boundary lines that come with size. The opinion leaders also rated these two characteristics third and fourth, respectively.

—*Save for a rainy day*. Although just 30 percent of the opinion leaders said the high performers they knew well had a rainy-day fund, 92 percent of the high performers said they had at least something set aside for lean times. Reserve funds may make perfect sense for managing an uncertain environment, but high performers may worry that such funds will somehow undermine their case for funding or will prompt questions about stewardship. As one would expect from size, smaller organizations said they have smaller funds, medium-size organizations have moderate funds, and larger organizations tend to have larger funds. The opinion leaders did not rate this as a shared characteristic of the nonprofits they knew well.

—*Stay flat*. Three-quarters of the executive directors reported three or fewer layers between the top and bottom of their organizations, with small organizations the flattest, and larger organizations the thickest. The opinion leaders rated this characteristic fifth.

—*Recruit a diverse staff*. Just over half of the high performers said they had a very diverse staff, which was defined as a staff made up of young and old, male and female, black, Latino and white staff members. The larger the organization, the more diverse the staff: 42 percent of the small high performers said their staff was very diverse, compared with 59 percent of the large high performers. The opinion leaders did not find this characteristic among at least half of the organizations they knew well.

The survey of high performers suggests growing difficulty in retaining talented staff, confirming the retention problems highlighted in my earlier study, *The New Public Service*. The nonprofit sector may be the destination of choice for graduates of the nation's leading public policy and administration graduate schools, but it has had the greatest difficulty holding staff over time. According to the 250 executives interviewed for this report, 41 percent of the high performers said their organizations were finding it very or somewhat difficult to retain staff, with the largest nonprofits having the greatest difficulty of all.

Small organizations can only motivate people so long with mission, however. As the head of a $1.5 million environmental advocacy group argued:

I am always struck by the turnover rates in most environmental groups. That generally translates to salaries and benefits—we all have kids and we all want them to go to college and live in decent housing and that sort of thing. There's only so much of the "beat-myself-on-the-back" stuff I'm going to be able to handle—I'll make some sacrifices but I'm not going to make a lot of them. So we have to pay real wages. We certainly have to pay what the Environmental Protection Agency pays or what consultants pay. We've made that transition here, but very few other organizations have, and, as a consequence, they have tremendous turnover. You lose all that institutional memory when those people leave, all their contacts and all the respect they've developed. We need to keep people around for a long time.

Perhaps that is why executive directors put such an emphasis on hiring and retaining talented staff as a prerequisite for high performance. "The main element is people," said the director of an art museum when asked what poorly performing nonprofits can do to increase performance. "You have to hire people that are mission driven, that are passionate about the mission. Then you have to establish a team approach, keeping everyone informed and training. You have to keep learning to make a nonprofit really work. With that type of work environment, you'll have people who hate to leave." The head of a volunteer placement agency agreed: "I am not the agency. The agency is made up of talented people who are going to do the work. And the better the talent, the better the synergy you are going to have and the more creative you're going to be. You have to set aside whatever ego you have and recognize that it's really the success of the whole that's going to make the difference."

Recruiting and retaining talented people also came up repeatedly when executive directors were asked about their greatest challenges in the long interviews. A theater director worried about the problems in getting applicants for entry-level jobs, for example. "Hiring new people has been really difficult in the last few years, and we've put out job descriptions and been very surprised at the small pool of applicants, particularly thinking back to five or ten years ago. It shows me that less and less people are interested in this field and that there isn't a normal structure where people can grow in the field and move up into positions of higher authority." An opera executive agreed: "The biggest problem we have is that we train our development people so well that others take them away. Former staff of ours are heading fund-raising departments at universities and hospitals all over the country. The difficulty is when you lose somebody, finding anybody good is very hard. We do a lot of in-house, on-the-job-training, which is time-consuming."

Arts organizations were hardly the only nonprofits hiring and holding talented staff. As the head of a homeless center argued, high-performing organizations work the people issue constantly:

> There's a difference between a motivator and a satisfier. And so we look at how we are nurturing our best people and how much attention, energy, and focus we are giving those best people—really giving people the ability to unleash their own creativity and really show some of their own leadership. The issue of retention is something you have to be on top of all the time. It starts with that hiring process.
>
> People want to be part of organizations that they perceive to be innovative, cutting edge, progressive, and really making a difference and doing things differently. One, you've got to get rid of bad people. There are some that are innovative, creative; they are getting the work done. There are some who are sort of putting in their time. And there are others that sow the seeds of discontent. The other thing is you invest in the direct management of really good people. Compensation in and of itself is not a motivator. The number one reason people stay with organizations is that they feel they have a really good working relationship with their direct supervisors.

As a future Center for Public Service report will show, the nonprofit sector has one of the most talented, committed work forces in the U.S. economy. But it is a work force that is both underpaid and under-resourced in comparison with both the private sector and government. The sector can rely on the psychic income produced by an intense commitment to mission for only so long, especially in a tight labor market.[3]

## Leadership

Leadership is one of the most difficult issues to explore with executives of any organization. It is almost impossible to formulate a survey question that will get an authoritarian, indecisive, inept, or inaccessible leader to acknowledge these behaviors, if only because there is a prevailing bias in American society for strong, empowering, smart, accessible leaders. It is just as difficult to arrive at a question that will get the humble, self-effacing leader to admit his or her style, again because doing so is contrary to the core philosophy of the leader-as-servant that such individuals follow.

This project addressed the tendency of leaders to overstate the importance of their own leadership in two ways. First, the survey asked about the leadership of high-performing nonprofits in general, the assumption being that leaders would be more honest in describing the leadership of other high-performing organizations than their own. Second, when the survey asked respondents about their leadership style, it did so by referring to the "management" of the organization in general, rather than the leadership style of the individual respondents. In theory, respondents were talking about themselves in answering both sets of questions, projecting their own leadership style onto other high-performing nonprofits and thinking of themselves when asked about the management of their organization.

These two approaches suggest that high-performing organizations share five leadership characteristics.

—*Foster open communications and motivate people.* Exactly 92 percent of the executive directors described communication between staff and management in their organizations as open and free flowing, reinforcing the earlier findings on teamwork and internal collaboration, while 91.6 percent also said it is very important for high-performing organization to have a leader who knows how to motivate people. The opinion leaders rated these two items first and second, too.

—*Clarify board/staff relationships.* The vast majority of the executives said the board understood its role in setting policy very well (72 percent), in general (62 percent), and in overseeing the organization's performance (61 percent). Smaller organizations were significantly less likely to report high levels of clarity, in part because small organizations tend to be younger organizations and still needing to develop a board. Exactly half of the executives of small organizations said the board understood its role in oversight performance, compared with 72 percent of the largest organizations. The opinion leaders rated board/staff relationships fourth.

—*Fund-raise.* Seventy-two percent of the executives said it is very important to have a leader who is a good fund-raiser, with no statistically significant differences by organization size. The opinion leaders rated this characteristic third.

—*Give the freedom to take risks.* Asked early in the survey about the characteristics of the leaders of high-performing organizations, two-thirds of respondents said that it is very important that high-performing organizations have a leader who encourages risk taking. Asked later in the survey about their own organizations, 59 percent said that the staff and management in their organization felt comfortable taking risks and trying new things. The opinion leaders did not find this characteristic in at least half of the high performers they knew well.

Much as these executives agreed on the need for open communications, risk taking, and internal collaboration, they were quite divided on how their organizations actually made decisions. Exactly half of the respondents said that their organization encourages the discussion of issues but reserves the final decisions for the executive director or board, while 43 percent said their organizations discuss issues until the staff arrive at a consensus about a decision.

The size and age of the organization have almost no bearing on decisionmaking style. Rather, the most significant predictor is whether the organization is headed by the founding director. Fifty-six percent of the high performers no longer headed by their founding director make decisions through the traditional hierarchical model, reserving final decisions for the executive director or board, while 53 percent of the high performers still headed by their founding director make decisions through a consensus-building model. Having built their organizations from the bottom up, founders appear willing to give up more control to the staff they recruited.

Executives were also asked two questions about the leadership traits of high-performance executives. First, they were asked about the general importance of having leaders who were decisive, honest, charismatic, faithful, and trusting. Honest emerged as the most important characteristic at 98 percent, followed by faithful at 85 percent, decisive at 79 percent, trusting at 75 percent, and charismatic at 35 percent. Like the opinion leaders, executives obviously had little enthusiasm for the charismatic leader. Executives at small, medium, and large organizations agreed on the rankings of honesty, faithfulness, and trust but disagreed sharply on decisiveness and charisma. The executives at small nonprofits were almost twice as likely as executives at large nonprofits to emphasize the importance of charisma (46 percent versus 26 percent), while the executives at large nonprofits were significantly more likely than executives at small organizations to emphasize decisiveness (92 percent versus 72 percent). Being charismatic may be essential for getting noticed as a small nonprofit, while being decisive may be critical for managing a large nonprofit.

**Table 4-3.** *The Characteristics of High-Performance Leaders*[a]

Percent

| Characteristic | Very important | Most important |
|---|---|---|
| Honest | 98 | 47 |
| Faithful | 85 | 14 |
| Decisive | 79 | 19 |
| Trusting | 75 | 13 |
| Charismatic | 35 | 5 |

a. N = 248.

Second, executives were asked to identify the most important of the five characteristics. As table 4-3 shows, honest emerges as the most important characteristic again, this time at 47 percent, followed by decisive (19 percent), faithful (14 percent), and trusting (13 percent) all at a statistical tie, and charismatic last, at just 5 percent.

Executives at small organizations were somewhat more likely than other groups to emphasize being decisive and the least likely to focus on honesty. None of this means that smaller nonprofits are dishonest, but given their lack of large reserve funds, they may have lower margins for error, which, in turn, may require quicker, more decisive decisionmaking.

A more precise image of the high-performing leader emerges from the long interviews with the subsample of twenty-five executives. Asked what skills have helped them be effective, two-fifths emphasized communication, a third focused on team building, and a fifth answered passion for mission, inclusiveness, management skills, knowing what's right, experience, honesty, and ability to bring out the best in people. "Integrity. Candor. Being willing to take risks. Having a good streak of perfectionism," the head of a social justice program answered. "And a willingness to see the big picture but to also hunker down and focus on the details. An ability to listen and really hear. An ability to own up to my own mistakes and not blame other people. And willingness to deal with the hard staff around race, class, and gender, and sexual orientation."

If not quite self-effacing, many of these executives refused to take credit for the high performance of their organizations. They were humble to an extent, unwilling to see themselves as indispensable to their organization's survival. "I'm personally not invested in seeing this organization become an empire," said the head of a technical assistance provider. "What I am invested in is achieving our mission. I am also deeply committed to openness and to not having any secrets. It forces me to be very aware of values and how I'm making decisions because I'm going to expose everything."

They also have a clear sense of their work in creating the conditions for others to succeed, whether by fund-raising, communicating, or just "walking the talk," as several said. The head of a dropout prevention program noted, "I have a real sense of what's right. What's right in terms of building an organization that respects the skills and integrity of the people working in it. Setting up systems to select staff that can work under those conditions and then setting up systems that can make sure we get things done at the same time as respecting the skills and integrity of the people. One hundred percent of my job is to make sure that staff have the conditions necessary for them to deliver their absolute best service. That's my job."

Whether they would call themselves decisive or reflective, trustworthy or charismatic, these executives also understand the importance of making choices. "We deleted a major program this year that had not been funded in its twenty-five years," said the head of a volunteer placement program. "Unbelievable. But the community saw it as one of the most important things we did. Not important enough to fund, mind you. And we finally had to say, sorry, we can't do it anymore. Oh, my God, you wouldn't believe the hate calls I got. I said I'd be happy to restore the program if they could find the money for it. At some point you have to say, look, we've gone to every funder, we've made formal presentations, and we can't do it anymore. It may be the best thing since sliced bread and the thing you like doing the most, but you just can't keep doing it."

Most important, these executives understood the importance of recruiting talented people and keeping the organization focused on mission as the prime motivator. Clearly, the journey toward higher performance is firmly rooted in talented people who are extraordinarily committed to their organization's mission. "Without passion and without being motivated, you might as well hang it up," said the director of a food center. "That's what drives people. Motivation is our fuel; it's our jet fuel."

## Internal Management Systems

Like the opinion leaders, the executive directors confirmed the importance of management systems for organizational performance. Although they certainly agreed on the individual pieces of a good management system—including accounting, job descriptions, and staff training—many of the executive directors talked about the need for these systems to keep the organization focused on the outside world. "One of the challenges I face here is getting our staff to look outside of ourselves," said the head of a national youth service organization. "What good ideas does the American Cancer Society have in the way they work with people? What good ideas does Fleet have? We need the ability to benchmark our work and do the right kind of boundary scanning so we know what's happening outside the confines of our movement. We're so focused on getting our job done that it's sometimes a great challenge to force ourselves to go out there and talk to five other organizations and find out what they're doing."

For these high-performing executives, internal systems do not serve the organization or act as a substitute for not knowing why the organization exists in the first place. Sometimes, therefore, the best thing to do is *not* measure, or *not* evaluate, or *not* focus on statistical outcomes. "The biggest concern I have is making sure we're measuring what we should be measuring and not just what someone else tells us to measure," said the director of a youth computer literacy program. "And that's particularly difficult now because there is so much focus on measuring a student's worth or a child's worth by their grades or by their test scores. We're trying very hard not to succumb to that. And it's not easy because there is so much momentum." Systems should serve the mission, not vice versa.

The 250 high performers shared four characteristics related to serving the mission:

—*Plan.* Echoing the opinion leaders' enthusiasm, 91 percent of the executives said their organizations had a strategic plan for the future. Of those plans, 44 percent were completed in the last year, 22 percent in the last one to two years, 12 percent in the last three to five years. The other 22 percent were being revised. In a word, the strategic plans were "fresh." Small, medium, and large organizations were equally likely, statistically speaking, to have plans in their files. The opinion leaders rated this characteristic third.

—*Be clear about responsibility.* Eighty-six percent of the executives said their organizations had position descriptions for the entire staff, with larger organizations more likely to have plans in place than small ones, in part because they have more formalized management systems in general. Although the survey did not ask how detailed these descriptions were, one suspects that the smaller organizations have broader job descriptions. The opinion leaders rated this second as well.

—*Use the board.* The opinion leaders were quite right in believing that high-performing nonprofits use their boards: 89 percent meet with their boards at least four times a year, and 35 percent meet nine times or more. The opinion leaders rated this first.

—*Track the funds.* Seventy-three percent of the executives said their organizations had an accounting system that made it very easy to get an accurate accounting of their expenses and revenues whenever they need it.

The high performers had a mixed inventory on other management systems. Just 46 percent of the executives said their organizations had information technology that could be described as very adequate, while 54 percent said that their organization provided some, a few, or no resources for staff training. In addition, only 43 percent said their organization used data to make decisions, and just 24 percent linked staff pay to performance.

Although few differences here were based on size, larger organizations were more likely to have the money to invest in pay for performance and to spend on training. One of the larger organizations that participated in the long interviews even reported having set aside $2,000 per person for training. "And we use it," the executive director said. "Every single person has to come up with a training plan. Every single person has a training goal for the year, and that's part of how their performance is judged at the end of the year." A second national youth-serving organization also talked about a significant increase in training, including "the career assistance networks, where we have experienced professions formally serving as mentors for young professionals, and an academy that recognizes professional development."

What all of these organizations did have were strategic plans, some developed through highly formalized, expensive processes led by consultants, others developed through informal, self-administered approaches. In the words of one executive director, "I think the whole thing comes down to planning. Far too often we don't begin with a blueprint of where we want to go. We think we have, because we have ideas. But far too often we do not put the ideas down on paper. We don't put numbers against them. We don't work out an action plan of how to get there. We tend to see a lot of organizations whether they are in the arts or elsewhere saying, 'We are going to be the best in the world,' and everybody applauds that and says, 'What an aim.' But that is only the beginning. You have to put that on page 100 of your plan and work backwards."

Even among those that undertake a formal planning process, there was a strong sense that traditional strategic planning models may be outdated.

A number of executive directors suggested that planning activities had to be regular, flexible, and more frequent. "The world is changing rapidly so I think the idea of a strategic plan lasting for five years doesn't work anymore," one said. "You are going to have to do it closer to two to three years. It is a constant thing. I think the old fashioned way of doing strategic planning isn't going to be very effective anymore with things changing so rapidly. You have to abbreviate that process and incorporate it almost annually with the activities that you do." The director of a small grassroots organization agreed:

> I am not sure, the kind of strategic planning that I have seen over the years is not terribly creative. And the process of arriving at it can be just, oh I don't know, excruciatingly dull. And the plan that you come out with at the end does not necessarily have things that really are creative or risk taking or they are sometimes so deliberate that I'm not sure that they make sense. And I think that the world, and I was saying this like a year ago, I think the world is changing so rapidly now because of technology. And now you know, I'm not sure that if we had a strategic plan now, it would make sense to use it.

The director of a capacity-building program noted that there are different models or "levels" of strategic planning, echoing a widely held belief among nonprofit assistance providers: that strategic planning (and other forms of capacity building) should involve outside assistance—a theme explored further in the next section.

> I think that there are different levels of strategic planning, but as an organization gets together and is able to capture the attention of key people in the organization, particularly the board, I think that whatever they do in that exercise is going to serve them well because it is likely that they are with outside facilitation they are going to look at their mission statement seriously, they are going to come together as a team and they are going to be focused on the same priorities. So, even if we don't get all we would like out of that process, I think a little bit of process can go a long way in a positive sense to strengthen an organization.

Others confirmed this more informal model. "I'm one of those people that looks at a strategic plan as a rolling plan," said the head of a national youth service organization. "You don't have a plan for three years and then say, 'OK, we're done.' We initiated our own planning process and have been in that mode for three years." The vice president of a rehabilitation program described this as the "loose-leaf binder approach." "If you start binding things, then they become the gospel instead of the guide. And situations change and circumstances change. But you've got to have a plan about where you are going to know why you didn't get there. If you just sort of start each day by saying 'I believe I'll go do good deeds,' you're not going to get anywhere. So, yes, we do strategic planning."

Strategic planning was closely linked to the effort to measure outcomes. "That's what's most critical to our ability to manage over time," the head of a community development agency noted. "We have to stay focused on the outcomes we care about. If our staff knows what we care about most, they're going to be focusing less on counting whether or not people showed up in meetings or attended 70 percent of the classes, and a lot more on the outcomes."

The caution among these executives was clear: strategic plans cannot be so tight that they limit opportunism and flexibility. The executive director of a community development organization put the goal of strategic planning simply: "We want to be informed opportunists. It's the way we do business here. And so that puts us max at a three-year horizon. Strategic planning is a way for us to talk about the most important things, but it's not to develop a hard and fast blueprint that we must follow."

The fear of being restrained led several of the executives to reject traditional planning altogether. Some were at relatively small nonprofits that simply could not afford the cost associated with hiring a strategic planning consultant, while others did not have the time to invest in the deep self assessment so often associated with successful planning. In many ways, the organizations that may most need strategic planning are those that can least afford it, because they are under such demand that they cannot bear the distraction or are growing so fast they cannot stop to take stock of their strengths, weaknesses, opportunities, and threats.

The vice president of an international relief agency agreed with the general portrait, but urged strategic planning nonetheless. "We're feeling pretty old as an organization . . . we're pretty mature. At a certain point, you become so 'project-ized' that people stop relating to the whole. A strategic plan helps you bring everybody back in and remind them about the overall mission, how they all fit into that mission." Interviewed in the week after September 11, the head of a volunteer placement agency explained the role of strategic planning as follows: "Certainly no one thought last Tuesday when we got up that something like that would happen and change our life. If we were an agency that said, 'Oh, no, sorry, we didn't have that on our work plan,' where would we be? We had to mobilize immediately. In addition to our regular work, we had an entirely new role to play. Strategic plans give you a framework, but they shouldn't be your nemesis."

## First Things First

As with the survey of opinion leaders, this survey of executives yields a long list of advice on the final destination, but less on where to begin. "My first piece of advice would be to take it slow," said the director of a local youth organization. "The other piece would be to hold your enthusiasm and make sure you're reinforcing the administrative side of your organization while you are building the service side. You really do have to balance it. You can put the organization into jeopardy because you're trying to do too much with too little." The head of a food program made the same point when asked what kinds of things should a nonprofit worry about first, second, then third. "The first one is to do your homework, including feasibility studies. We are very, very careful to tell people that there's no sense in reinventing the wheel. If someone else is doing something similar to what you want to do, seek their advice. The people in our industry are very willing and open to give advice. So we did that first. We did lots and lots of homework."

Once past the homework, however, nonprofits have to make choices. The question then becomes whether to start strategic planning, hire a fund-raiser, fire the founding director, buy new computers, or any one of dozens of possibilities in dealing with the external environment, internal structure, leadership, and internal systems.

Like the opinion leaders, executives were asked the first step a similar nonprofit organization should take to become a high-performing organization: work on becoming well managed or work on increasing their program impacts? Fifty-nine percent of the executives said first work on becoming well managed, another 31 percent said first work on increasing program impacts, and 9 percent answered "both." These answers track almost perfectly with the sample of opinion leaders, creating a two-to-one margin for strengthening the administrative infrastructure as a first step toward higher performance.

Once again, size helps explain the answer. Executives at smaller and medium-size organizations were more likely to put the focus on being well managed than executives at large organizations, while those at the latter were more likely to emphasize programmatic impacts than those at the former. Larger organizations are more likely to have the administrative infrastructure already in place and may need to refresh their program agenda, while small organizations may have highly energized programs without the infrastructure.

Once past this question, the executives were asked how to improve a below-average performing organization. This effort to define pathways to high performance involved three steps: identifying targets of improvement, forcing a choice on four targets, and asking whether strategic planning was the place to start.

### Targets of Improvement

The executives were first asked to evaluate each of the four areas of organizational life separately. Asked how important it is for a below-average performing organization to improve its external relationships, internal structure, leadership, and internal management systems, 92 percent of the 250 executives rated leadership as very important, followed by internal management systems at 82 percent, internal structure at 68 percent, and external relationships at 64 percent.

There was no difference between small, medium-size, and large organizations on the leadership question, but significant differences on the other three. Executives at small and medium-size organizations were more likely than those at large nonprofits to emphasize the need to manage external relationships and internal structure, while executives at large ones were more likely to emphasize administrative infrastructure.

Not surprisingly, the executives who earlier stressed becoming well managed first were more likely to say that internal structure and internal management systems were very important targets for improving poorly performing nonprofits than their colleagues who had emphasized improving program impacts first. Whereas 74 percent of the former said internal structure was very important, only 54 percent of the latter agreed.

### Forced Choices Again

Once past this gateway question, the executives were asked which of the four areas was most important for a below-average performing organization to improve first. As with the opinion leaders, the answer was clear: 71 percent of the executives put leadership first, followed by internal structure and internal management systems at 12 percent each, and external relationships at just 3 percent.

Once again, executives who said that organizations should start the journey to high performance by working on management were significantly more likely to focus on internal structure and systems, while those who said the journey should start with program impacts emphasized leadership. The management-first group was four times more likely than the program-first group to focus on internal structure and systems, while the program-first executives put leadership fifteen percentage points higher than the management-first executives.

As noted earlier, the executives at small organizations were less likely than their peers to put the emphasis on leadership. Just 53 percent recommended that below-average organizations start with leadership, compared with 80 percent and 83 percent of the executives at medium-size and large nonprofits, respectively.

One explanation involves the presence of founding directors. Smaller organizations are more likely than either medium-size or large organizations to have their founding director still in place, which helps explain the lack of concern for leadership among their executives. Not surprisingly, 56 percent of the executives in organizations with their founding director still in place put leadership at the top of their list, compared with 73 percent of the executives in organizations that no longer had their founder at the helm.

Having identified the most important starting point for improvement, the 250 executives were then asked to identify the most important component of external relationships, internal structure, leadership, or internal management systems to work on specifically. Their top-ten list is as follows: know how to motivate people (51 respondents, or 20 percent, picked this specific step); have a clear understanding with executives and boards about their respective roles (43 respondents, or 17 percent); have a participatory style of management (20 respondents, or 8 percent); have few barriers between organizational units and encourage risk taking (tied at 9 respondents, or 4 percent); give staff authority to make routine decisions on their own and encourage staff to work in teams (tied at 8 respondents, or 3 percent); have few layers of management between the top and bottom of the organization (4 respondents, or 2 percent); collaborate with other organizations (3 respondents, or 1 percent); regularly survey clients regarding programs and services, measure results or outcomes, fund-raise, be charismatic, have position descriptions for staff, hold regular board meetings (tied at 2 respondents, or 1 percent).

Like the list compiled for opinion leaders, this one sums to far less than 100 percent. Seven respondents did not answer the question, another eighteen said "none," and forty-seven offered their own suggestions. Although respondents were able to pinpoint the broad target of improvement, they were less willing to give the specific coordinates. As in the opinion leaders' list, here, too, people become the number one starting point for improvement when individual items on the list are combined by subject. Thirty-five percent of the executives focused on the need for below-average organizations to find leaders who know how to motivate people, have a participatory style of management, encourage staff to work in teams, and delegate authority to make routine decisions. Another 20 percent pinpointed the need to set clear expectations by clarifying board/staff relationships, measuring results, writing position descriptions for staff, surveying clients regularly, and holding regular board meetings. And 7 percent emphasized the need for organizational restructuring by lowering the barriers between organizational units and staying flat.

## Planning Can Wait

Strategic planning is the one area where the opinion leaders and executives disagreed on the pathways to improvement. Whereas 9 percent of the opinion leaders said a below-average nonprofit should start with strategic planning, not one of the executives agreed. It is not because the executives avoid strategic planning. Recall that the vast majority were either currently engaged in strategic planning or had a plan that was less than two years old.

Nor is it because the executives believe strategic planning is an unimportant exercise. The long interviews reveal a deep belief in using strategic planning to discipline a high-performing organization. Asked if she would recommend strategic planning to other organizations as a way of improving performance, the head of a food center said: "Absolutely. Absolutely. It's a great way to do a report card. And it's not just a report card. We almost use it as a syllabus. During our monthly staff meetings, we go back and redefine our marks. Are we spending too much time on a no-win situation? Do we have the right amount of energy and staffing to make it happen? Are we going about it the right way?" "You've got to start with the dream," said the head of an opera company. "But then there is the good old hard work of an action plan to get to that dream. Numbers that go into the plan. It is all very well to have a budget, but you need source and application. And sourcing the money is often not done, particularly in the arts."

Rather, the lack of enthusiasm for strategic planning as a starting point appears to be rooted in the fact that these high performers take it so seriously. Strategic planning is not a frivolous exercise that one does to set course. "It can lay you wide open," said the executive director of a food center. "It can make the leader very vulnerable, and the staff feel inadequate. It can be a very scary thing to do." The vice president of a coalition of international relief agencies agreed. "It's a pain in the neck. It's very easy to say, yeah, let's go do a strategic plan, but it is a big job if you do it correctly. It's onerous, demanding of the staff, takes a lot of time. The last thing anyone is going to want to do is a strategic plan." Asked to explain the lack of enthusiasm among his colleagues, the head of a theater mused that "maybe the thinking was that you have to be at a certain level of success before you can plan. If you're planning in total disarray, you won't get anywhere, which would save everyone a lot of time and effort."

Done well, strategic planning is expensive and often exhausting and demands an extraordinary commitment from the board, executives, staff, and volunteers. Done poorly, it can be distracting at best, destructive at worst. It can create false expectations about the future and laundry lists of impossible goals. It can also expose basic tensions within the organization. "Strategic planning can be an extraordinarily stupid exercise," said the director of an environmental group, "especially when I'm dealing with a group of people who don't read and don't listen. They expect to sit down at the table and tell us what we should be doing. The last time I looked, I didn't see any of them with waders on taking samples or reading the monitoring results. This is not Dow Chemical."

Reading the in-depth interviews, these executives view strategic planning more as a tool for *sustaining* high performance, and less as a starting point for achieving excellence. As the head of the opera company said, "So many things change. In our case, a lot of our money comes from individuals, and individuals die. You have to sit down every year and objectively, painfully, look at our major donors and create holes in our forward budgeting in anticipation of the deaths of certain people. And then we have to replace that money with new donors."

## The Board as a Bridge

Much as they supported strategic planning for their own organizations, these executives saw little value in developing elaborate plans that cannot be implemented. They worried more about basic needs such as computers, accounting systems, staff training, and fund-raising, almost to the point of using a hierarchy of needs to describe the journey toward improvement, starting with worries about shelter, heat, and light early in the change process to concerns about self-actualization of staff later on.

For many of the executives interviewed at length, the board was the bridge between basic organizational needs and mission.[4] And everything starts with the choice of lumber, one director argued.

> If you're building your obituary and you just want to be able to list a bunch of boards, don't include the center. And if you're already serving on eleven boards, don't make us be your twelfth one. Maybe you would like to serve on our board at another time that would be better for you, because we do have expectation for attendance. We're seeking you because you bring a particular knowledge of community, a particular skill, a particular background, a particular something, that makes you important to the organization. And therefore, know that we're not just looking for board members. And we're not going to just put your name on our letterhead.

The interviews also made it clear that board members of these high-performing nonprofits were extremely dedicated and hardworking. As one executive director said, "They put in tremendous amounts of time. We have nine board meetings a year plus committee meetings, which is a little unusual, but that is sort of a tradition and when we try to cut that back people say, 'Well, if you only had meetings every other month and I missed one, it would be four months and I would not know what the hell was going on.' That creates some work for the staff, but it certainly keeps the board in touch."

Board members of high-performing nonprofits are dedicated, and in some cases, hands-on. The director of a young nonprofit explained that "until recently, the last couple of months, the board has been a working board. They have been in here, up to their elbows cleaning and painting and I mean, we're calling it sweat equity. They have been here. They have written policy. They have implemented plans. They are our backbone."

Clearly, these executive directors are convinced that a strong board is vital to their organizational effectiveness. When asked how important their boards had been in the success of their organizations, the majority of directors said their boards had been *very* important, and only three out of the twenty-five said their board had not played a significant role. For example, the executive director of a large national organization explained that her first question to herself upon taking over as leader was, "What steps do we need to take to build what I would feel and what we could all point to as the absolute best non-profit board in America." When asked about the importance of her board, another leader answered: "Incredibly. One of those ingredients for success. I'm not a Pollyanna type but the first time I went to a retreat-type thing I was stunned to hear that most EDs didn't like their board. I was like, 'oh?' Mine is incredible. Sincerely they are. I use them a lot."

Others pointed to board quality as a significant cause for decline. "If I could identify one element that is the most significant in the spiraling downward of any nonprofit organization, it is the lack of a clear understanding between board and staff," said the head of an art museum. "The big danger is that board members try to run the place, but don't have that expertise in the field. I have seen it all across the United States. You have to be very sensitive and proactive in this area. If the relationship deteriorates, the whole nonprofit suffers."

The role of the board, however, varies greatly with size and age of the organization. The director of one small hunger program said of its working board: "They're giving us things that we would have to spend money on. Accounting. Legal advice. Development policy." But as organizations age, that kind of engagement can create enormous conflict with the staff, pointed out another executive director:

We started out with a bunch of middle managers on the board that gave us $15 a year and ducked when anybody shot. You have to get them out of the way. They haven't been very important in the past but will be very important in the next stage. We can't be so dependent on contracts and grants. I'd love to have a $10 to $20 million endowment, and I do see a sizable reserve fund. The board has been instrumental in the last year in beginning to raise that money. And that's beyond my scope. I can't ask the rich guys for that money.

This executive director was hardly alone in wanting to improve his board. Eight of his twenty-five fellow executives said they were encouraging their boards to take a larger fund-raising role, while three more talked about the need for broad improvement. "In the beginning, our board sort of rubber-stamped our decisions," said the head of a community health agency. "It was a board of do-gooders who didn't really have any money or expertise. We're now working to bring more political people into the picture, as well as people alert to the politics that we have to deal with in Medicaid."

Moreover, many of the executives noted that board relationships must be forged time and again as new members and chairs come and go. "Every time I get a new board president I need to redefine what the expectation is," said the head of a volunteer placement agency. "I didn't do that well enough one time and had a horrible year because the new chair was unable to verbalize her expectations. By the time I figured out I wasn't meeting them, she was ready to fire me." Even well-established organizations can need help setting clear boundaries between board and staff. "I have seen agencies that are very highly developed get a new board leader who wants things done differently for no other reason except the way they operate is different," the volunteer agency head continued. "And suddenly there is a witch hunt to get rid of the executive. You have got to set clear expectations every time there is a change."

## People First

This focus on board development reinforces a central finding from the survey of executives: people and mission are essential for building a high-performing organization. Asked why they had a reputation for high performance, half of the executives interviewed in depth pointed to the staff, and nearly two-fifths focused on clarity of mission. And when asked what advice they would give to a nonprofit leader who was trying to build a high-performing organization, 60 percent said "hire good people," and just over half said "focus on mission." Without talented people, it is difficult to imagine how even the most carefully crafted mission can succeed; but without a carefully crafted mission, talented people will not remain engaged for long.

That is certainly how the head of a dropout prevention program viewed the combination: "Find the best staff that you can afford and hire them, because it's the staff that touches children and family lives. That's the first thing. The second thing is to make sure that all of your programs have clear goals that are measurable. And the third thing is get out of the way. Let the staff do their work." The vice president of a rehabilitation center also focused on people and mission. "I don't want to get into management 101 when it comes to personnel issues, but I think nothing is more critical than getting the right people into the right jobs doing the right things and being treated right. I don't know that everything has to be real complicated to make sense."

The job description for the staff of a high-performing nonprofit is simple: WANTED: SELF-STARTERS COMMITTED TO CAUSE. "We're too small to have somebody who can't take care of business on a daily basis without being watched," the director of an environmental advocacy group argued. "We're too small to hire anybody who's not a self-starter." A theater director described his organization's search process as follows:

> You look for people who are interested in whatever your organization does. You want them to be loyal and interested and not just doing a job. When we recently hired a development and financial management person, we found that we just couldn't compete with the for-profit sector even with upgrading our salary. So we found a financial manager who was a certified public accountant with a Master's of Business Administration who had studied acting at Northwestern and still takes classes in improv. And we found a development person who had gone to school in costume design. So for us, it is finding people who have a love for the art form.

The key here is not just to find talented people wherever they might be, but to find talented people who identify with the organization's mission. "Everybody here is passionate about the work of nonprofits and most come from the nonprofit world," said the director of a technical assistance agency. "We're here because we want to strengthen the sector, and that's very, very clear. The norm here is how does our work help or hinder that mission. Without that anchoring post, you start to flounder."

Even as they focused on their staffs and boards, these leaders of high performers recognized their own role in achieving and sustaining excellence. For them, the job of the leader involved five central activities:

—*Communicate*. Asked what skills had helped them be effective, two-fifths of the executives in the long interviews focused on communication. "Communication is number one, two, and three," said the vice president of a rehabilitation program. "I started out with a degree in journalism, and that has served me very well in being able to communicate both internally and externally." The executive director of a religious education agency argued that everything starts with the vision: "You have to find people who hold the vision no matter what. You don't have to hold it tight. In fact, the tighter you hold it, the less it can breathe. You should hold it loosely, with love and with faith, and then others will gravitate to it."

—*Build relationships*. Like the opinion leaders, the executives stressed all aspects of team building and collaboration, both inside their organizations and outside. "I've worked hard to develop trust and respect between the national organization and local affiliates," said the head of a national youth service agency. "Our relationship has never been better. Last year we passed through more than $40 million to our local affiliates. We've gotten contributions of hardware and software, and created great value for our members, which has helped us align everyone behind our plan for the future."

—*Stay focused*. As already mentioned, high-performing organizations keep tightly focused on mission. "Tops on the list would be visionary," said the head of a food center about her own skills. "I've been accused of being a fanatic. Bulldog in nature. Motivator. Efficient. Goal-oriented. Outcome-oriented. About as compassionate as all get out. Weird combination, huh?" That may be a weird combination, but it is very familiar in the deep conversations with high-performing leaders.

—*Get out of the way*. Part of recruiting talented people is giving them the freedom to do their jobs, even if that heightens the risk of mistakes. "It's important to be able to step back and let people make their own decisions, even if you think it's not the decision you would make," said a theater director. "Otherwise, your people won't grow and they'll always wait for the okay. You want them to make decisions and prosper, not call you every minute while you're on vacation."

—*Be ready to say "no."* Even as they push authority downward and encourage teamwork, the leaders of high-performing organizations recognize their role in making final decisions, particularly in saying "no." "When something is stuck, it's my job to unstick it," said the head of a drop-out prevention program. "You can't be afraid for the buck to stop here."

## Looking for Help

Being open to new ideas is also part of the job description for a high-performing leader. Although the executives interviewed for this study certainly understood the difference between the private and nonprofit sector, most were willing to take a good idea from any sector. "I encourage the executive leadership here to be alert to anything that might help us become more effective," said the head of a dropout prevention project. "That means going to workshops, seminars, reading the trade publications, talking with colleagues. You take all of that learning, the *Harvard Business Review*, other books that come out, and lay them out on the table and see what fits with us. Most of the time what we find is that we're already a lot more efficient than for-profits."

This ecumenicalism is evident in executive views of management reform. Although the 250 executives were predictably skeptical about mergers and external reviews, where 43 percent and 67 percent, respectively, said the reforms had added nothing at all to their performance, they were much more likely than the opinion leaders to endorse most of the reforms that have moved through the nonprofit sector in recent years. As table 4-4 shows, 51 percent said that the encouragement to do more strategic planning had improved their own organization's performance a great deal, followed by an increased openness to using standard business tools at 42 percent, more funding for capacity building at 38 percent, and increased emphasis on outcomes measurement and the encouragement to stay longer in their jobs tied at 37 percent. (See table 3-2 for the parallel answers from the opinion leaders.)

All of the executives were not equally enthusiastic about the reforms. Executives at larger nonprofits were less enthusiastic about the encouragement to collaborate, no doubt because they are at less agile organizations. They are also more satisfied about measuring outcomes, no doubt because they have the resources and expertise to make such measurements. Smaller nonprofits appear to benefit more from collaboration, perhaps as a pathway toward getting larger through learning and eventual mergers, and are less likely to have the capacity to measure outcomes.

Not surprisingly, the encouragement to collaborate was seen as much less helpful among founding executives: just 27 percent said the reform had helped their organizations a great deal, compared with 48 percent of nonfounding executives. Founding directors were also less likely to embrace mergers and alliances. Just 10 percent said the reform had

Table 4-4. *What Has Helped: How Much Have Various Reforms Improved Performance?*[a]

Percent

| Reform | Great deal | Fair amount | Not too much | Nothing at all |
|---|---|---|---|---|
| The creation of management standards | 20 | 34 | 22 | 20 |
| The encouragement to collaborate with other nonprofits | 37 | 36 | 20 | 8 |
| Making nonprofits more open to the public and media | 19 | 35 | 22 | 22 |
| Reducing duplication and overlap among nonprofits through mergers and alliances | 16 | 20 | 18 | 43 |
| Strengthening external reviews | 2 | 8 | 20 | 67 |
| The encouragement to do more strategic planning | 51 | 33 | 8 | 7 |
| Giving executive directors greater access to training | 31 | 38 | 15 | 13 |
| Encouraging executive directors to stay longer in their jobs | 37 | 24 | 10 | 24 |
| Encouraging more funding for capacity building | 38 | 27 | 16 | 16 |
| Increased emphasis on outcomes measurement | 37 | 42 | 12 | 8 |
| Management assistance grants | 12 | 20 | 15 | 49 |
| Increased openness to using standard business tools | 42 | 40 | 11 | 6 |
| More active donor involvement | 24 | 34 | 18 | 24 |

a. N = 250.

helped their organizations a great deal, compared with 28 percent of the nonfounding directors.

The 250 executives may have been more open to ideas than the opinion leaders expected, but they were less hopeful about the sources of help. When asked which organizations had contributed the most to helping improve their organization's performance, most executives answered, "none of the above." As table 4-5 shows, only 15 percent said that providers of technical assistance had provided a great deal of help, followed by 14 percent for associations of nonprofits, and 8 percent each for government, management service organizations, and external rating organizations. (See table 3-3 for the parallel answers from the opinion leaders.)

Table 4-5. *Who Will Help: Who Has Helped Improve Nonprofit Sector Performance Most?*[a]

Percent

| Source | Great deal | Fair amount | Not too much | Nothing at all |
|---|---|---|---|---|
| Foundations | 27 | 39 | 22 | 13 |
| Government | 8 | 21 | 26 | 45 |
| Graduate schools | 4 | 20 | 33 | 41 |
| Management service organizations | 8 | 25 | 34 | 30 |
| External rating organizations | 8 | 18 | 24 | 46 |
| Providers of technical assistance | 15 | 47 | 28 | 10 |
| Associations of nonprofits | 14 | 44 | 27 | 15 |

a. N = 250.

When one includes the respondents who answered that a given organization had helped a fair amount, the small and large organizations differ significantly on three sources of help. First, by a margin of 71 percent to 57 percent, the smaller organizations were more likely to say that foundations had helped a great deal or fair amount, no doubt because many of the capacity-building programs around the country are targeted at smaller organizations. Second, by a margin of 34 percent to 14 percent, larger organizations were more likely to say that graduate schools had provided a great deal or fair amount of help, possibly because they had the resources to both recruit staff from those schools and send their executives to training programs. Finally, by a margin of 65 percent to 47 percent, smaller organizations were more likely to say that associations of nonprofits had provided a great deal or fair amount of help, perhaps because that is where so many turn for help in initial start-up training.

The greatest difference with the opinion leaders came on the role of foundations in improving performance. Just 8 percent of the opinion leaders said foundations had provided a great deal of help in the past, compared with 27 percent of the executives. Whether for good or ill, the executives believe that funding is essential for improving management.

## Conclusion

Some may see this chapter as a ringing endorsement for new leadership. After all, what could be a faster way to high performance than finding that special leader who combines tenacity with vision, decisiveness with faith, even if it means firing the current executive? Nothing could be a greater misreading of the data.

The executives are not saying "change the leader," but "change the leader's work." Few believe that a single person can make a nonprofit excel, and few think that finding the mythical heroic leader is the answer to all that ails nonprofit organizations. To the contrary, these executives clearly believe that it is the leader's job to create the conditions under which others in the organization can succeed, whether by writing position descriptions for the staff, breaking down the barriers between units, coaching staff on taking risks, raising money, or measuring outcomes.

This does not mean individual leaders are insignificant. There is ample evidence that leaders do matter greatly, particularly in reminding their organizations about mission. But the measure of a good leader is not to be found in his or her willingness to work eighty-hour weeks, raise every last dollar, or install each new system. It is in the leader's ability to drive a sense of mission down through the organization, upward into the board, and outward into the community, and to be willing to do whatever it takes to enable the organization to follow that mission effectively.

That kind of leadership comes in many shapes and sizes, from the mythical heroic leader to mild-mannered administrator. But heroic or unassuming, the leader's work remains the same: make it easy for the organization in sum to be greater than its parts. That can be done with sizzle or self-effacement, charisma or quietude, but it is the central challenge for moving toward high performance.

## CHAPTER FIVE

# Pathways to Excellence

It is tempting to conclude that the journey toward high performance begins with but a single step. However, the reality is much more complicated. Achieving and sustaining high performance is hard work and involves the same tenacity, endurance, risk taking, trial and error, and stubbornness that produces innovation and program success. Building a high-performing organization takes time and energy, not to mention money, and can be just as disruptive at times as a funding crisis, leadership transition, or spike in demand.

There is a cost to producing program impacts *and* improving management simultaneously, not the least of which is double, triple, and quadruple duty among board members, executives, and staffs. Most nonprofits cannot shut down for six months to retool their plants or install a new computer system. Nor can they stop feeding the hungry, nursing the ill, protecting the environment, educating the children, or developing the community to prepare a strategic plan or design a new organizational structure.

It is easy to understand why some nonprofits would avoid the journey altogether. In the short run at least, it may be easier to produce outcomes in spite of the external isolation, internal bureaucracy, poorly functioning boards, or antiquated management systems than to launch the kind of effort that will eventually produce ordinary excellence.

In the long run, however, the benefits from doing the double, triple, and quadruple duty are clear. High-performing nonprofits still work very hard, but they usually work easier. Instead of grinding themselves against poor systems, wondering whether they make any difference at all, worrying about the next financial crisis, waiting for their computers to crash, or wondering whether their phones still work, high-performing nonprofits have the luxury of concentrating on their reason for being.

As noted at the outset of this report, nonprofits can have high performance the hard way or the easy way, with or without decent salaries for their staff, with or without reasonable measures of their work, and with or without effective management systems, access to training, participatory leadership, or a reserve fund. Even the most understaffed, underresourced nonprofit can still deliver the goods and services, but it will not do so for long.

## An Inventory of Agreements

The opinion leaders and executives shared more agreements than disagreements on the characteristics and starting points for improving performance. Indeed, the two samples disagreed on just a dozen of the nearly 100 answers given in the two surveys. The opinion leaders were more likely than the executives to say that an organization can be very effective in achieving its program goals but not be well managed, and less likely to say most nonprofit organizations are better managed today than they were five years ago.

The rest of the disagreements focused on proposals for improving nonprofit performance. Opinion leaders were less enthusiastic than executives about the value of collaboration, mergers, external reviews, outcomes measurement, using standard business tools, and donor involvement for improving the sector's performance, but more supportive of more training for executive directors, more funding for capacity building, and management assistance grants. As such, the executives were more likely to focus on management as the starting point for high performance than the opinion leaders, and more willing perhaps to take any tool that might help improve their impacts. The executives were also less likely to see the value in strategic planning as a starting point for high performance.

Once past this handful of disagreements, the opinion leaders and executives were in close agreement on the importance of management, the characteristics of high-performing organizations, and the first steps toward improvement. Both samples agreed that they would advise organizations to begin the journey toward higher performance by first working on becoming well managed, and that an organization can be very well managed and still not achieve its program goals.

Both samples also agreed on the external relationships, internal structure, leadership, and internal management systems of high-performing organizations. On external relationships, both focused on the need to collaborate, measure, diversify, generate revenue, and know the client; on internal structure, both emphasized the need to stay as flat as possible, push authority downward, work in teams and collaborate internally, and exploit technology to the best of their ability; on leadership, both samples underlined the need to clarify board/staff roles, motivate people, foster open communications, encourage at least some level of risk taking, and keep the money flowing through fund-raising; and on internal management systems, both embraced the need for strategic planning, clarifying responsibilities, using the board, and tracking funds.

Both samples were underwhelmed by the need for charismatic leaders but clearly concerned about the growing problems recruiting staff, leaders, and boards. Both samples were also underwhelmed by the state of the information technology in most nonprofits, suggesting a clear need for capacity building. The two samples agreed that strengthening leadership is the starting point for improvement, not by finding the mythical heroic leader, but by changing the leader's work to involve clear board/staff responsibilities, learning how to motivate people, and giving people in the organization the freedom to do their jobs well.

## Mapping the Journey to High Performance

The journey to high performance may not start with just one step, but it does start with some level of self-awareness. Simply put, each nonprofit must map its own journey to high performance. Much as it might admire the systems and reserve fund of a $30 million think tank, a $500,000 neighborhood builder might be better off looking at similar organizations for advice. Similarly, much as it might admire the edginess and agility of a $500,000 neighborhood builder, a $30 million think tank might be better advised to look at other large nonprofits for insights into how to improve.

Toward that end, each nonprofit must decide how it will winnow the list of possible destinations and strategies to fit its own aspirations, assets, and history. Some nonprofits will want to winnow the list through the eyes of opinion leaders who said there were few high performers among the organizations they knew well. Others will want to reframe the data through the eyes of executives at small, young nonprofits versus those at large, old nonprofits. Still others will want to see what the data show through the eyes of founders and nonfounders.

### Setting a Higher Bar

The opinion leaders varied greatly in the number and percentage of high performers they knew. Some saw high performance among most of the organizations they knew well, while others saw high performance among only some or a few.

Generally speaking, the more organizations the opinion leaders knew well, the fewer they were willing to describe as high performers. Either these opinion leaders raised the bar as they encountered more organizations, had more data on which to impose a normal grading curve, or were just more stubborn about naming high performers. Only 28 percent of these opinion leaders said that most nonprofits were better managed today than they were five years ago, compared with 42 percent of the opinion leaders who saw high performance in most of the organizations they knew well. Whatever the reason, these more selective respondents can be used as an informal control group for winnowing the list of characteristics and strategies. (See table 5-1 for an inventory of significant differences between the opinion leaders based on the proportion of high performers among the organizations they said they knew well.)

Opinion leaders who saw fewer high performers among the organizations they knew well were much more likely to describe those nonprofits as "collaborative," and much less likely to describe high performers as "innovative." They were also more likely to know high performers who were very small, but less likely to know high performers that were very large. They were also less likely to say that the leaders of high performers are good fund-raisers or charismatic, less likely to see demographically diverse staffs, pay for performance, or adequate information technology, and much more likely to put the emphasis on having a participatory management style as the first step toward improvement.

All in all, these more selective respondents saw less sizzle in the high performers they know, and much more external and internal collaboration. Theirs is a portrait of high performance that is activated from all corners of the organization by leaders who use whatever tools they can find to focus on improvement. They are just as likely as other opinion

**Table 5-1.** *The High Performers That Opinion Leaders Know*[a]

Percent

| Question and response | How many well-known organizations are high performers? | | |
| --- | --- | --- | --- |
| | Most | Some | Few |
| "Innovative" describes high-performing nonprofits very well | 75 | 59 | 62 |
| "Collaborative" describes high-performing nonprofits very well | 52 | 44 | 62 |
| Most nonprofits are better managed today than they were five years ago | 42 | 25 | 22 |
| Are any of high performers you know well very small (< $500,000)? | 58 | 73 | 74 |
| Are any of high performers large (> $10 million)? | 50 | 50 | 38 |
| Most high performers rely on volunteers to deliver at least some of their services | 46 | 43 | 57 |
| Only a few high performers have an environment that can be described as heavily regulated | 44 | 30 | 30 |
| Most have demographically diverse staffs | 54 | 42 | 32 |
| Most or some are having trouble retaining staff | 56 | 75 | 69 |
| Most or some are having trouble retaining leaders | 39 | 57 | 49 |
| Most or some are having trouble retaining board members | 39 | 43 | 57 |
| Most have experienced rapid growth | 40 | 35 | 50 |
| Most have leaders who are good fund-raisers | 77 | 58 | 66 |
| Most have leaders who can be described as charismatic | 44 | 26 | 34 |
| Most link pay to performance | 23 | 11 | 15 |
| Most have adequate information technology | 46 | 34 | 32 |
| Among respondents who said leadership was the most important area for an organization performing below average to improve first, percentage who said having a participatory management style was the most important component of leadership to improve first | 7 | 15 | 26 |
| Graduate schools contribute a great deal or fair amount to improving nonprofit performance | 46 | 62 | 62 |
| Associations of nonprofits contribute a great deal to improving nonprofit performance | 29 | 23 | 9 |
| The creation of management standards has contributed a great deal over the past few years to improving nonprofit performance | 8 | 13 | 18 |
| Strengthening external reviews has contributed a great deal | 12 | 2 | 3 |
| The encouragement to do more strategic planning has contributed a great deal | 42 | 48 | 28 |
| Increased openness to using standard business tools or techniques has contributed a great deal | 21 | 19 | 32 |

a. N = 52 for most, 118 for some, and 74 for few.

leaders to see strategic plans in the organizations they admire, but much less likely to see planning as the answer to poor performance. More than any other group, these opinion leaders put the focus on the organization as a whole, not a charismatic, fund-raising leader, innovative program, or a strategic plan.

Yet even as they emphasized the importance of people, these opinion leaders were clearly worried about the sector's ability to retain the talent it needs. Not only were they less likely than other opinion leaders to see the diversity upon which so much innovation relies, they also reported that the high performers they knew were having serious problems retaining staff, leaders, and board members. It is difficult not to depend on the charismatic leader when organizations are having trouble retaining talent at all levels.

## Age and Size

By themselves, age and size are significant predictors of what high-performing nonprofits do. But together, they show two very different approaches to improvement among young/small organizations and old/large ones. Although all small organizations are not young and all large organizations are not medium-size or large, the relationship between age and size is clear. Of the 90 small nonprofits (budget less than $1 million) in this study, 46 were fifteen years old or younger, 28 were between fifteen years and thirty years old, and just 16 were more than thirty years old; of the 100 medium-size nonprofits (budget of $2 million to $10 million), just 19 were fifteen years old or younger, 39 were between fifteen years and thirty years old, and 42 were more than thirty years old; and of the 58 large nonprofits (budget over $10 million), 46 were over thirty years old and just 4 were under the age of fifteen.

As table 5-2 shows, young/small organizations behave very differently from large/old organizations, which suggests very different strategies for achieving and sustaining high performance at different stages of the organizational life cycle.[1] Getting noticed and managing growth are the statistically significant challenges for young/small nonprofits. Hence these organizations were more likely to focus on the need for charismatic leaders, working on management first, and improving internal organizational structure. Their need for systems, access to training, and flexible resources is also clear.

In contrast, renewal and red tape are the key issues for large/old nonprofits. These organizations were more likely to focus on the need for

## Table 5-2. *The Combined Impact of Size and Age*[a]

Percent

| Question and response | Young + small | Old + medium + large |
|---|---|---|
| | **Size and age of nonprofit** | |
| Very important for leader of a high-performing nonprofit to be "decisive" | 72 | 88 |
| Very important for leader of a high-performing nonprofit to be "charismatic" | 57 | 30 |
| Strongly or somewhat agree that most nonprofit organizations are better managed today than they were five years ago | 63 | 86 |
| Similar nonprofit should first work on increasing program impacts | 20 | 36 |
| Own organization has a diversified funding base to a large extent | 41 | 61 |
| Own organization relies on volunteers to a large extent | 54 | 35 |
| Own organization has experienced significant growth in demand to a large extent | 87 | 65 |
| "Competitive" describes the general environment very or somewhat well | 33 | 72 |
| "Heavily regulated" describes the general environment very or somewhat well | 30 | 49 |
| Own organization has one or few layers of management between top and bottom | 43 | 16 |
| Own organization has four or more layers | 2 | 36 |
| Own organization has a large reserve fund | 15 | 30 |
| Own organization has very or somewhat difficult time retaining staff | 22 | 57 |
| Own organization has position descriptions for all of staff | 76 | 92 |
| Own organization has a lot of programs or resources for staff training | 35 | 56 |
| Organization performing below average should work on internal organizational structure first | 22 | 3 |
| Organization performing below average should work on leadership first | 52 | 83 |
| Graduate schools have contributed a great deal or fair amount to improving own organization's performance | 9 | 35 |
| Strengthening external reviews have contributed a great deal or fair amount to own organization's performance | 2 | 14 |
| An increased emphasis on outcomes measurement has contributed a great deal or fair amount to own organization's performance | 72 | 88 |

a. N = 46 for young + small, 88 for old + medium + large.

decisive leaders, increasing program impacts, and dealing with competition. They also appeared to feel much greater pressure to confront the complacency embedded in hierarchy and formalized procedures. Whereas small/young nonprofits need help building the plane while flying it, old/large organizations need help taking it apart without crashing it. It is particularly important to note the problems large/old organizations were having retaining staff. Even though the vast majority of nonprofit organizations are small, the vast majority of nonprofit employees work at large organizations. To the extent that the old/large organizations profiled here speak for other old/large organizations, the nonprofit sector appears to be well on its way to a human capital crisis.

### The Founder's Dilemma

A final way to sort the data is through the eyes of founders and nonfounders in organizations that could still have their founding director, meaning organizations under thirty years of age. As table 5-3 shows, organizations with founding directors still in place were not that different from organizations with nonfounders.

The table also suggests that having a founder still in place is both an advantage and a liability for a high-performing nonprofit. On the one hand, founders are more likely to emphasize the kind of participatory decisionmaking style that so many executive directors admired and are less likely to see leadership as the answer to what ails below-average performing organizations. On the other hand, these founders seemed much harsher about the role of technical assistance providers and associations of nonprofits in improving their organization's performance, suggesting perhaps a "not-invented-here" approach to reform.

## Nonprofit-Like Hearts and Minds

Mapping the journey to higher performance also involves the core values of the organization and its leadership style. Some nonprofit leaders are more reflective in nature, while others are faster to reach a decision; some organizations put their energy into new ideas and opportunism, while others focus on building long partnerships and steady growth. Although nonprofits can sometimes contain all of the above, there appear to be several different models of how to combine organizations (hearts) with leaders (minds).

**Table 5-3.** *Founders and Nonfounders*[a]

Percent

| Question and response | Founder still in charge | Nonfounder in charge |
|---|---|---|
| Most important characteristic of high performing nonprofit is "rigorous" | 10 | 1 |
| Organization's leadership style is to discuss issues until consensus is reached | 53 | 36 |
| Own organization has position descriptions for all of its staff | 70 | 90 |
| Very important for organization performing below average to improve leadership | 85 | 97 |
| Organization performing below average should work on leadership first | 56 | 73 |
| Providers of technical assistance have contributed nothing at all to own organization's performance | 24 | 5 |
| Associations of nonprofits have contributed nothing at all to own organization's performance | 25 | 9 |
| Reducing duplication and overlap has improved own organization's performance a great deal | 10 | 28 |

a. N = 59 for founder organizations, 86 for nonfounder organizations.
Samples include only organizations that are less than thirty years old.

Recall that in the survey executives were asked to choose the most important characteristic of a high-performing nonprofit organization and the most important characteristic of a nonprofit leader. As noted in chapter 4, being innovative was rated the most important characteristic of a high-performing nonprofit, followed by being principled, entrepreneurial, collaborative, resilient, and rigorous. In turn, being honest was rated the most important characteristic of a leader of a high-performing nonprofit, followed by being decisive, faithful, trusting, and charismatic.

The lists generate at least two models each of the high-performing organization and leader. Statistically, the words "principled" and "collaborative" go together as descriptions of the high- performing organization, or "heart," as do the words "entrepreneurial" or "innovative," while "resilient" and "rigorous" are unrelated to any other words. In turn, the words "decisive" and "charismatic" go together as descriptions of a high-performing leader, or "mind," as do the words "honest," "faithful," or "trustworthy." Table 5-4 shows these words also produce a long

## Table 5-4. Hearts and Minds[a]

Percent

| Question and response | Heart | | | Mind |
|---|---|---|---|---|
| | Principled + collaborative | Innovative + entrepreneurial | Honest, faithful, trusting | Decisive + charismatic |
| Very important for leader of nonprofit to be "decisive" | 77 | 78 | 72 | 98 |
| Very important for leader of nonprofit to be "charismatic" | 26 | 42 | 27 | 58 |
| Very important for leader of nonprofit to be a good fund-raiser | 63 | 79 | 66 | 88 |
| Very important for leader of nonprofit to encourage risk taking | 61 | 74 | 67 | 66 |
| Own organization collaborates with other organizations to a large extent | 79 | 75 | 79 | 64 |
| Own organization has a diversified funding base to a large extent | 45 | 64 | 56 | 56 |
| "Competitive" describes the general environment very or somewhat well | 51 | 66 | 58 | 68 |
| Only somewhat agree that own organization encourages staff to work in teams | 14 | 20 | 14 | 27 |
| Own organization has a large reserve fund | 21 | 20 | 22 | 10 |
| Own organization has a very difficult or somewhat difficult time recruiting board members | 14 | 12 | 13 | 5 |
| Organization's leadership style is to reserve final decisions for the executive director | 50 | 50 | 46 | 63 |
| Own organization provides a lot of programs or resources for staff training | 46 | 49 | 49 | 32 |
| Own organization's accounting system makes it very easy to get an accurate accounting | 78 | 68 | 77 | 63 |

| | | | |
|---|---|---|---|
| Organization performing below average should improve organizational structure first | 12 | 14 | 9 | 20 |
| Among respondents who said organization structure should be improved first, percentage who said having few barriers between units was the most important component to improve first | 42 | 27 | 50 | 8 |
| Graduate schools have nothing at all to contribute to improving own organization's performance | 48 | 33 | 40 | 42 |
| Providers of technical assistance have a great deal or fair amount to contribute to improving performance | 75 | 58 | 64 | 56 |
| Strategic planning has contributed a great deal or fair amount to own organization's performance | 84 | 86 | 83 | 93 |
| Strategic planning has contributed not too much or nothing at all | 15 | 14 | 17 | 7 |
| Encouraging foundations to provide more funding for capacity building has contributed a great deal or fair amount | 60 | 69 | 61 | 75 |
| Management assistance grants have not contributed at all | 48 | 49 | 54 | 37 |

a. $N = 91$ for principled + collaborative; $N = 138$ for innovative + entrepreneurial; $N = 175$ for honest, trusting, faithful; $N = 58$ for decisive + charismatic. Italicized entries denote statistically significant differences using a Z-test of percentages.

list of statistically significant differences in the characteristics and strategies of high-performing nonprofits.

Executives who selected principled or collaborative as the most important characteristic of a high-performing nonprofit were significantly less likely to focus on the charismatic, fund-raising, risk-taking leader, and more likely to emphasize accounting systems, reducing the barriers between organizational units, and the role of technical assistance providers in improving their own organizations. In contrast, executives who selected entrepreneurial or innovative were significantly more likely to emphasize the role of the leader in pursuing high performance, while emphasizing the importance of a diversified funding base, the competitive nature of the environment, and the general sense that a high performer must go it alone somehow.

Executives who selected honest, faithful, or trusting as the most important characteristic of the leader of a high-performing nonprofit were also quite different from their peers. Again, they were less likely to focus on the charismatic, fund-raising executive, less likely to characterize the environment as competitive, and less likely to report that their organizations reserved final decisions for the executive director. These executives were much more likely, however, to put the emphasis on building organizational capacity, whether through collaborating with the outside world, building a large reserve fund, providing resources for staff training, building an accurate accounting system, or reducing the barriers between internal units.

In contrast, executives who selected decisive or charismatic as the most important characteristic of the leader of a high-performing nonprofit were more likely to describe a leader-centered organization. They were more likely than their peers to emphasize the charismatic, fund-raising, decisive leader who makes the final decisions, perhaps because they do not have the reserve fund, accounting system, and staff training that their peers have. It is easy, these executives might say, to be collaborative, reflective, and organization-centered when an organization has a large reserve fund and operates in a less competitive environment.

The question here is whether there is any special combination of organization and leadership that is most conducive to high performance. The best one can do is note that the executives who said that being honest was the most important characteristic for leaders of high-performing organizations were statistically more likely to say being collaborative and principled were the most important characteristics of a high-performing organization, while those who said being faithful was the most important leadership characteristic were also more likely to say being principled was the most important organizational characteristic. Four models of the high-performing nonprofit emerge when the word choices are sorted.[2]

—*Principled/decisive*. This high-performing organization has an organization-centered structure headed by a decisive leader. Fourteen executives, or 6 percent, combined collaborative or principled with decisive or charismatic.

—*Principled/reflective*. This high-performing organization also has an organization-centered structure with a more reflective leader. Eighty-five executives, or 34 percent, combined collaborative or principled with honest, faithful, or trusting.

—*Entrepreneurial/decisive*. This high-performing organization has a leader-centered structure with a decisive leadership style. Thirty-one executives, 12 percent, combined entrepreneurial or innovative with decisive or charismatic.

—*Entrepreneurial/reflective*. This high-performing organization also has a leader-centered structure with a reflective leadership style. Seventy-seven respondents, 31 percent, combined entrepreneurial or innovative with honest, faithful, or trusting.

Note that the first combination, which some might call the nonprofit heart/for-profit mind, showed up among just 6 percent of the 250 executives, while the for-profit heart/nonprofit mind emerged as the more attractive option with 31 percent. If there is to be more entrepreneurial attitude in the organization, these respondents would prefer a more reflective leader at the helm.

As table 5-5 shows, these combinations produce different assets and liabilities for the high-performing organization. Organizations that prefer the entrepreneurial/decisive model may underinvest in the capacity needed to sustain high performance over time, for example, while those that embrace the principled/reflective model may underexploit opportunities for innovation.

Executives who favored the pure entrepreneurial/decisive model had a very distinctive view of high-performing organizations compared with that of their peers. On the question of external relationships, they were more likely to say their own organization had a diversified funding base, existed in a highly competitive environment, and had experienced significant growth in demand. On internal structure, they were more likely to say staff had the authority to make routine decisions, in part because

**Table 5-5. Organizations and Leaders**[a]

Percent

| | Organization/leader combination | | |
| --- | --- | --- | --- |
| Question and response | Entrepreneurial/ decisive | Principled/ reflective | Mixed |
| Very important for leader of a high-performing nonprofit to be "decisive" | 100 | 74 | 77 |
| Very important for leader of a high-performing nonprofit to be "charismatic" | 65 | 23 | 36 |
| Very important for leader of a high-performing nonprofit to be a good fund-raiser | 90 | 59 | 77 |
| Strongly agree that most nonprofits are better managed today than they were five years ago | 58 | 30 | 32 |
| Own organization has a diversified funding base to a large extent | 61 | 47 | 60 |
| Own organization has experienced significant growth in demand to a large extent | 90 | 76 | 78 |
| "Competitive" describes general environment of own organization very or somewhat well | 74 | 51 | 61 |
| "Heavily regulated" describes general environment of own organization very or somewhat well | 23 | 37 | 41 |
| Own organization has two or fewer layers of management between the top and bottom | 54 | 52 | 43 |
| Staff make routine decisions on their own | 90 | 80 | 75 |
| Strongly agree that own organization encourages staff to work in teams | 68 | 87 | 81 |
| Own organization's information technology very adequate | 23 | 44 | 53 |
| Own organization's accounting system makes it very easy to get an accurate accounting of expenses and revenues whenever needed | 55 | 80 | 72 |
| The government has contributed a great deal or fair amount to improving own organization's performance | 35 | 37 | 22 |

| | | | |
|---|---|---|---|
| External rating organizations have contributed a great deal or fair amount to improving own organization's performance | 45 | 29 | 19 |
| Providers of technical assistance have contributed a great deal or fair amount to own organization's performance | 58 | 74 | 55 |
| Associations of nonprofits have contributed a great deal to own organization's performance | 29 | 13 | 11 |
| The encouragement to collaborate has contributed a great deal to own organization's performance | 35 | 48 | 31 |
| The encouragement to do more strategic planning has contributed a great deal or fair amount to own organization's performance | 100 | 84 | 80 |
| Encouraging executive directors to stay in their jobs longer has contributed nothing or not too much to own organization's performance | 48 | 28 | 33 |
| Management assistance grants have contributed a great deal or fair amount to own organization's performance | 48 | 28 | 29 |
| Increased openness to using standard business tools or techniques has contributed a great deal to own organization's performance | 65 | 41 | 37 |
| More active donor oversight has contributed nothing at all to own organization's performance | 6 | 23 | 29 |

a. N = 31 for entrepreneurial/decisive, 86 for principled/reflective, 133 for mixed.

their organizations are so flat, but less likely to say the organization encourages staff to work in teams. On leadership, they were more likely to put the emphasis on being decisive, charismatic, and a good fundraiser. On internal systems, they were less likely to rate their information technology or accounting systems as highly as their peers. Not surprisingly, these executives were more enthusiastic about strategic planning (encouraging executive directors to stay in their jobs), more open about using business tools, and more welcoming of external oversight, whether through external rating systems or greater donor involvement. Reading between the lines of data, they seem to have a preference for going it alone in a highly competitive environment.

Executives who favored the pure principled/reflective model had a very different image of the world and their organizations than their entrepreneurial/decisive colleagues. On the question of external relationships, they were less likely to have the diversified funding of their peers and more likely to describe their environment as heavily regulated. On internal structure, they worked in taller organizations that encouraged staff to work in teams. On leadership, they were far less likely than the executives who embraced an entrepreneurial/decisive model to emphasize the decisive, charismatic, fund-raising leader. On internal systems, they favored their information technology and accounting systems much more and were much more likely to say that providers of technical assistance and collaboration had improved their organizations. Again, reading between the lines of the data, they seem to have a longer-term, community-oriented view of their operations and seem more willing to use their resources to invest in the internal systems to make endurance possible.

Executives who preferred a mixed model (principled/decisive or entrepreneurial/reflective) tended to agree with their principled/reflective peers on most aspects of organizational life. Although they viewed fund-raising and the diversified base it produces as somewhat more important, and collaboration as somewhat less important, they did not let the entrepreneurial or decisive side of their thinking dominate their views of the high-performing nonprofit.

This analysis suggests again that there is no one best way to design or lead a high-performing nonprofit organization. Rather, there are different pathways to high performance, each with its own strengths and weaknesses. The entrepreneurial/decisive nonprofit tends to be more agile, and perhaps a bit more innovative, but to have weaker internal systems and to be less able to collaborate. In contrast, the principled/reflective non-profit tends to be steadier, perhaps a bit less opportunistic, but weaker at making quick decisions.

## Conclusion

Nonprofit organizations vary greatly in their characteristics and strategies in taking the first step toward higher performance. Some start with the leader, others with the accounting system, and still others with a call for help. But wherever they start, they never stop. There is no final destination, a point at which a high-performing nonprofit stops improving.

This commitment to continuous improvement is, in fact, at the core of the definition of what it means to be a nonprofit-like organization. Having started the journey to higher performance, a nonprofit-like organization keeps the pressure on no matter where it happens to be in the journey. It updates its strategic plan regularly, invests in staff training, continues to evaluate and measure its performance, modernizes its systems, and continues to exploit opportunities. Regardless of the competition, or lack thereof, nonprofit-like organizations constantly raise the bar on their own performance. They do not look outside for the pressure to improve, but to their own mission.

Answering this call for improvement is essential for building confidence in the wake of September 11. Whatever the ultimate impact of the Red Cross and United Way controversies, the nonprofit sector is being challenged as never before to prove its stewardship, effectiveness, and efficiency. Even when confidence rebounds, as it almost certainly will given past trends, the pressure from outside the sector will not let up. Private firms will continue to cut into traditional nonprofit fields, while faith-based organizations will continue to press for a share of lucrative government contracts. Whether the coming months and years will produce winnowing, withering, or awakening is entirely up to the nonprofit sectors and its advocates.

# *Opinion Leaders' Survey*

N = 250 executives of high-performing nonprofits
N = 85 members of Grantmakers for Effective Organizations
N = 80 members of ARNOVA
N = 85 members of the Alliance for Nonprofit Management

Margin of error ±6% for total sample

Q1.  To start, I have a couple of questions about you. On average, what percentage of your professional time do you spend (Insert)?

| | Less than 25% | 25% to 50% | More than 50% | Don't know | Refused |
|---|---|---|---|---|---|
| a. providing technical assistance to nonprofits as a consultant | | | | | |
| total | 55 | 17 | 25 | 2 | 1 |
| GEO | 61 | 21 | 15 | 2 | 0 |
| ARNOVA | 78 | 9 | 13 | 1 | 0 |
| alliance | 28 | 20 | 47 | 2 | 2 |
| b. helping nonprofits improve their performance through grant making and other philanthropic activities | | | | | |
| total | 57 | 16 | 23 | 2 | 2 |
| GEO | 28 | 27 | 44 | 1 | 0 |
| ARNOVA | 79 | 10 | 6 | 4 | 1 |
| alliance | 65 | 12 | 18 | 2 | 4 |
| c. doing research and teaching about nonprofit organizations as a scholar | | | | | |
| total | 70 | 14 | 15 | 1 | * |
| GEO | 96 | 2 | 0 | 0 | 1 |
| ARNOVA | 43 | 23 | 33 | 3 | 0 |
| alliance | 68 | 19 | 13 | 0 | 0 |

Q2.   How familiar are you with the literature on organizational performance—very familiar, somewhat familiar, not too familiar, or not familiar at all?

| total | GEO | ARNOVA | alliance | |
|---|---|---|---|---|
| 41 | 100 | 27 | 59 | Very familiar |
| 48 | 0 | 57 | 37 | Somewhat familiar |
| 10 | 0 | 16 | 0 | Not too familiar |
| 1 | 0 | 0 | 4 | Not familiar at all |
| 0 | 0 | 0 | 0 | Don't know |
| 0 | 0 | 0 | 0 | Refused |
| 73 | 2 | 44 | 27 | Based on those who spend at least 25% of time doing research or teaching |

Q3.   How much of your knowledge about nonprofits comes from personal experience with nonprofits—most, some, or only a little of your knowledge?

| total | GEO | ARNOVA | alliance | |
|---|---|---|---|---|
| 74 | 87 | 49 | 84 | Most |
| 24 | 12 | 45 | 15 | Some |
| 3 | 1 | 6 | 1 | Only a little |
| 0 | 0 | 0 | 0 | Don't know |
| 0 | 0 | 0 | 0 | Refused |

Q4.   Words often have somewhat different meanings to people. When you hear the words "organizational effectiveness" what does it mean to you?

| total | GEO | ARNOVA | alliance | |
|---|---|---|---|---|
| 99 | 100 | 100 | 98 | Gave Response |
| 1 | 0 | 0 | 2 | Don't know |
| 0 | 0 | 0 | 0 | Refused |

Q5.  How well do the following words describe exemplary nonprofit organizations, that is high-performing organizations. Let's start with (Insert). Does this word describe high-performing organizations very well, somewhat well, not too well, or not well at all?

| | Very well | Somewhat well | Not too well | Not well at all | Don't know | Refused |
|---|---|---|---|---|---|---|
| a. rigorous | | | | | | |
| total | 40 | 42 | 7 | 5 | 5 | 0 |
| GEO | 49 | 40 | 4 | 2 | 5 | 0 |
| ARNOVA | 38 | 36 | 13 | 8 | 6 | 0 |
| alliance | 34 | 51 | 6 | 6 | 4 | 0 |
| b. innovative | | | | | | |
| total | 64 | 32 | 2 | 2 | 0 | 0 |
| GEO | 62 | 33 | 4 | 1 | 0 | 0 |
| ARNOVA | 60 | 38 | 3 | 0 | 0 | 0 |
| alliance | 71 | 25 | 1 | 4 | 0 | 0 |
| c. collaborative | | | | | | |
| total | 51 | 44 | 4 | * | 1 | 0 |
| GEO | 46 | 49 | 4 | 0 | 1 | 0 |
| ARNOVA | 50 | 43 | 6 | 0 | 1 | 0 |
| alliance | 56 | 39 | 4 | 1 | 0 | 0 |
| d. principled | | | | | | |
| total | 76 | 19 | 4 | 0 | 2 | 0 |
| GEO | 68 | 26 | 5 | 0 | 1 | 0 |
| ARNOVA | 78 | 18 | 4 | 0 | 1 | 0 |
| alliance | 81 | 14 | 2 | 0 | 2 | 0 |
| e. resilient | | | | | | |
| total | 72 | 25 | 2 | 0 | * | * |
| GEO | 75 | 22 | 1 | 0 | 1 | 0 |
| ARNOVA | 61 | 35 | 3 | 0 | 0 | 1 |
| alliance | 80 | 18 | 2 | 0 | 0 | 0 |
| f. entrepreneurial | | | | | | |
| total | 37 | 52 | 8 | 3 | * | 0 |
| GEO | 29 | 61 | 7 | 2 | 0 | 0 |
| ARNOVA | 34 | 51 | 13 | 3 | 0 | 0 |
| alliance | 48 | 42 | 5 | 4 | 1 | 0 |

Q6.   Please tell me if you strongly agree, somewhat agree, somewhat disagree, or strongly disagree with these statements:

|  | Strongly agree | Somewhat agree | Somewhat disagree | Strongly disagree | Don't know | Refused |
|---|---|---|---|---|---|---|
| a. An organization can be very well managed and still not achieve its program goals | | | | | | |
| total | 44 | 35 | 10 | 10 | 1 | * |
| GEO | 42 | 36 | 6 | 13 | 1 | 1 |
| ARNOVA | 49 | 33 | 9 | 9 | 1 | 0 |
| alliance | 41 | 35 | 16 | 7 | 0 | 0 |
| b. An ogranziation can be very effective in achieving its program goals but not be well managed | | | | | | |
| total | 27 | 41 | 20 | 12 | * | 0 |
| GEO | 32 | 35 | 19 | 13 | 1 | 0 |
| ARNOVA | 20 | 46 | 21 | 13 | 0 | 0 |
| alliance | 28 | 42 | 20 | 9 | 0 | 0 |
| c. Most nonprofit organizations are better managed today than they were five years ago | | | | | | |
| total | 28 | 49 | 11 | 4 | 7 | 2 |
| GEO | 24 | 48 | 14 | 5 | 6 | 4 |
| ARNOVA | 28 | 48 | 9 | 5 | 10 | 1 |
| alliance | 32 | 51 | 9 | 1 | 6 | 1 |

Q7.   If you were advising an organization on how to become a high-performing organization, would you tell them to first work on becoming well managed or to work on increasing their program impacts?

| total | GEO | ARNOVA | alliance | |
|---|---|---|---|---|
| 57 | 61 | 46 | 64 | First work on becoming well managed |
| 21 | 12 | 38 | 14 | Work on increasing program impacts |
| 18 | 24 | 11 | 18 | Both (Volunteered) |
| 1 | 1 | 1 | 0 | Don't know |
| 4 | 2 | 4 | 5 | Refused |

Q8.   Just your best guess, how many nonprofits did you work with last year, that is in 2000?

| total | GEO | ARNOVA | alliance | |
|---|---|---|---|---|
| 95.90 | 104.01 | 41.73 | 139.30 | Mean |
| 0 | 0 | 0 | 0 | Don't know |
| * | 0 | 0 | 1 | Refused |

Q9.   And thinking about all the nonprofits you know, how many do you know well—just your best guess?

| total | GEO | ARNOVA | alliance | |
|---|---|---|---|---|
| 22.40 | 28.40 | 15.17 | 25.861 | Mean |
| 1 | 1 | 0 | 1 | Don't know |
| 0 | 0 | 0 | 0 | Refused |

Q10.   Now thinking about the overall performance level of the organizations you know well, how many are high-performing organizations—most, some, only a few, or none?

| total | GEO | ARNOVA | alliance | |
|---|---|---|---|---|
| 21 | 20 | 25 | 18 | Most |
| 48 | 52 | 41 | 49 | Some |
| 30 | 27 | 30 | 32 | Only a few |
| 1 | 0 | 3 | 1 | None |
| * | 0 | 1 | 0 | Don't know |
| 0 | 0 | 0 | 0 | Refused |
| 248 | 84 | 80 | 84 | Based on those who know at least one nonprofit well |

Q11.   Do any of the high-performing organizations you know well focus on (Insert), or not?

Based on those who know at least a few high-performing organizations,

Total n = 244, GEO n = 84, ARNOVA n = 77, alliance n = 83.

| | Yes | No | Don't know | Refused |
|---|---|---|---|---|
| a. the arts and culture | | | | |
| total | 52 | 48 | 0 | 0 |
| GEO | 50 | 50 | 0 | 0 |
| ARNOVA | 44 | 56 | 0 | 0 |
| alliance | 63 | 37 | 0 | 0 |
| b. the environment | | | | |
| total | 41 | 59 | * | 0 |
| GEO | 42 | 57 | 1 | 0 |
| ARNOVA | 38 | 62 | 0 | 0 |
| alliance | 43 | 57 | 0 | 0 |
| c. community development | | | | |
| total | 66 | 34 | * | 0 |
| GEO | 69 | 30 | 1 | 0 |
| ARNOVA | 58 | 42 | 0 | 0 |
| alliance | 70 | 30 | 0 | 0 |

(continued)

Q11.   Do any of the high-performing organizations you know well focus on (Insert), or not? *(Continued)*

|  | Yes | No | Don't know | Refused |
|---|---|---|---|---|
| d. housing/homelessness | | | | |
| total | 59 | 41 | 1 | 0 |
| GEO | 67 | 33 | 0 | 0 |
| ARNOVA | 38 | 61 | 1 | 0 |
| alliance | 70 | 29 | 1 | 0 |
| e. nutrition or hunger | | | | |
| total | 36 | 63 | 1 | 0 |
| GEO | 40 | 58 | 1 | 0 |
| ARNOVA | 27 | 71 | 1 | 0 |
| alliance | 40 | 59 | 1 | 0 |
| f. education | | | | |
| total | 75 | 24 | 1 | 0 |
| GEO | 69 | 27 | 4 | 0 |
| ARNOVA | 78 | 22 | 0 | 0 |
| alliance | 78 | 22 | 0 | 0 |
| g. children and youth | | | | |
| total | 81 | 19 | * | 0 |
| GEO | 86 | 13 | 1 | 0 |
| ARNOVA | 68 | 32 | 0 | 0 |
| alliance | 88 | 12 | 0 | 0 |
| h. general human services | | | | |
| total | 73 | 27 | 0 | * |
| GEO | 71 | 27 | 0 | 1 |
| ARNOVA | 65 | 35 | 0 | 0 |
| alliance | 82 | 18 | 0 | 0 |
| i. health | | | | |
| total | 63 | 37 | * | 0 |
| GEO | 73 | 27 | 0 | 0 |
| ARNOVA | 45 | 53 | 1 | 0 |
| alliance | 69 | 31 | 0 | 0 |
| j. job training | | | | |
| total | 50 | 48 | 1 | 0 |
| GEO | 61 | 38 | 1 | 0 |
| ARNOVA | 43 | 56 | 1 | 0 |
| alliance | 47 | 52 | 1 | 0 |

Q12.   What about the size of the high-performing organizations you know well. Are any of them (Insert), or not?

Based on those who know at least a few high performing organizations,

Total n = 244, GEO n = 84, ARNOVA n = 77, alliance n = 83.

| | Yes | No | Don't know | Refused |
|---|---|---|---|---|
| a. very small, less than $500,000 annual budget | | | | |
| total | 70 | 29 | 1 | 0 |
| GEO | 75 | 25 | 0 | 0 |
| ARNOVA | 65 | 32 | 3 | 0 |
| alliance | 70 | 30 | 0 | 0 |
| b. small, between $500,000 and a million | | | | |
| total | 78 | 20 | 2 | 0 |
| GEO | 87 | 12 | 1 | 0 |
| ARNOVA | 64 | 32 | 4 | 0 |
| alliance | 83 | 17 | 0 | 0 |
| c. medium, more than a million and less than $10 million | | | | |
| total | 86 | 13 | 1 | 0 |
| GEO | 90 | 10 | 0 | 0 |
| ARNOVA | 77 | 21 | 3 | 0 |
| alliance | 92 | 8 | 0 | 0 |
| d. large, more than $10 million | | | | |
| total | 46 | 52 | 2 | 0 |
| GEO | 42 | 56 | 2 | 0 |
| ARNOVA | 42 | 56 | 3 | 0 |
| alliance | 55 | 45 | 0 | 0 |

Q13.   Of the high-performing organizations you know well, have any been in operation (Insert), or not?

Based on those who know at least a few high-performing organizations,

Total n = 244, GEO n = 84, ARNOVA n = 77, alliance n = 83.

|  | Yes | No | Don't know | Refused |
|---|---|---|---|---|
| a. less than 7 years | | | | |
| total | 47 | 50 | 3 | 0 |
| GEO | 60 | 37 | 4 | 0 |
| ARNOVA | 27 | 71 | 1 | 0 |
| alliance | 52 | 43 | 5 | 0 |
| b. between 7 and 15 years | | | | |
| total | 85 | 14 | 2 | 0 |
| GEO | 92 | 7 | 1 | 0 |
| ARNOVA | 74 | 25 | 1 | 0 |
| alliance | 88 | 10 | 2 | 0 |
| c. over 15 years | | | | |
| total | 87 | 10 | 3 | 0 |
| GEO | 89 | 7 | 4 | 0 |
| ARNOVA | 81 | 17 | 3 | 0 |
| alliance | 90 | 7 | 2 | 0 |

Q14.   Let's talk about how these high-performing organizations deal with their *external relationships,* that is, the outside world. How many of the high-performing organizations that you know well (Insert)—most, some, only a few or none?

Based on those who know at least a few high-performing organizations,

Total n = 244, GEO n = 84, ARNOVA n = 77, alliance n = 83.

|  | Most | Some | Only a few | None | Don't know | Refused |
|---|---|---|---|---|---|---|
| a. collaborate with other organizations | | | | | | |
| total | 70 | 24 | 6 | 0 | 0 | 0 |
| GEO | 74 | 21 | 5 | 0 | 0 | 0 |
| ARNOVA | 77 | 18 | 5 | 0 | 0 | 0 |
| alliance | 59 | 33 | 8 | 0 | 0 | 0 |
| b. have a diversified funding base | | | | | | |
| total | 64 | 26 | 8 | 1 | 2 | 0 |
| GEO | 68 | 24 | 6 | 0 | 2 | 0 |
| ARNOVA | 65 | 21 | 9 | 4 | 1 | 0 |
| alliance | 58 | 33 | 8 | 0 | 1 | 0 |

(continued)

Q14.  Let's talk about how these high-performing organizations deal with their *external relationships,* that is, the outside world. How many of the high-performing organizations that you know well (Insert)—most, some, only a few or none? *(Continued)*

| | Most | Some | Only a few | None | Don't know | Refused |
|---|---|---|---|---|---|---|
| c. rely on volunteers to deliver at least some of their services | | | | | | |
| total | 48 | 30 | 18 | 3 | 1 | 0 |
| GEO | 46 | 32 | 17 | 2 | 2 | 0 |
| ARNOVA | 55 | 26 | 17 | 3 | 0 | 0 |
| alliance | 43 | 31 | 20 | 5 | 0 | 0 |
| d. regularly survey their clients regarding programs and services | | | | | | |
| total | 41 | 33 | 19 | 2 | 6 | 0 |
| GEO | 36 | 37 | 19 | 1 | 7 | 0 |
| ARNOVA | 42 | 32 | 16 | 4 | 6 | 0 |
| alliance | 45 | 30 | 22 | 0 | 4 | 0 |
| e. measure the results or outcomes of what they do | | | | | | |
| total | 56 | 29 | 12 | 2 | 1 | 0 |
| GEO | 57 | 29 | 13 | 1 | 0 | 0 |
| ARNOVA | 61 | 29 | 8 | 3 | 0 | 0 |
| alliance | 51 | 30 | 16 | 1 | 2 | 0 |
| f. have experienced significant growth in demand for their programs and services over the past five years | | | | | | |
| total | 64 | 32 | 4 | 1 | * | 0 |
| GEO | 68 | 29 | 4 | 0 | 0 | 0 |
| ARNOVA | 61 | 34 | 3 | 1 | 1 | 0 |
| alliance | 61 | 33 | 5 | 1 | 0 | 0 |
| g. generate at least some unrestricted revenue | | | | | | |
| total | 68 | 22 | 7 | 1 | 2 | 0 |
| GEO | 63 | 24 | 10 | 1 | 2 | 0 |
| ARNOVA | 64 | 23 | 5 | 3 | 5 | 0 |
| alliance | 76 | 19 | 5 | 0 | 0 | 0 |

Q15.   Does (Insert) describe the general environment of most of the high-performing organizations you know, some, only a few, or none?

Based on those who know at least a few high performing organizations,

Total n = 244, GEO n = 84, ARNOVA n = 77, alliance n = 83.

| | Most | Some | Only a few | None | Don't know | Refused |
|---|---|---|---|---|---|---|
| a. turbulent | | | | | | |
| total | 23 | 28 | 31 | 17 | 1 | * |
| GEO | 12 | 31 | 43 | 13 | 0 | 1 |
| ARNOVA | 36 | 27 | 18 | 18 | 0 | 0 |
| alliance | 23 | 25 | 30 | 19 | 2 | 0 |
| b. competitive | | | | | | |
| total | 45 | 32 | 17 | 5 | * | 1 |
| GEO | 39 | 35 | 18 | 7 | 1 | 0 |
| ARNOVA | 43 | 34 | 21 | 3 | 0 | 0 |
| alliance | 52 | 28 | 13 | 5 | 0 | 2 |
| c. heavily regulated | | | | | | |
| total | 10 | 31 | 33 | 22 | 3 | 1 |
| GEO | 8 | 32 | 31 | 24 | 4 | 1 |
| ARNOVA | 14 | 25 | 38 | 22 | 0 | 1 |
| alliance | 7 | 35 | 30 | 20 | 6 | 1 |

Q16.   What's the *internal organizational structure* like of the high-performing organizations you know well? How many (Insert)—most, some, only a few, or none?

Based on those who know at least a few high-performing organizations,

Total n = 244, GEO n = 84, ARNOVA n = 77, alliance n = 83.

| | Most | Some | Only a few | None | Don't know | Refused |
|---|---|---|---|---|---|---|
| a. have few layers of management between the top and bottom of the organization | | | | | | |
| total | 51 | 34 | 11 | 2 | 1 | 0 |
| GEO | 55 | 32 | 12 | 0 | 1 | 0 |
| ARNOVA | 56 | 27 | 14 | 1 | 1 | 0 |
| alliance | 43 | 42 | 8 | 5 | 1 | 0 |
| b. have demographically diverse staffs—young and old, male and female, black, Latino, and white staffs | | | | | | |
| total | 42 | 43 | 12 | 2 | 1 | 1 |
| GEO | 42 | 42 | 14 | 1 | 1 | 0 |
| ARNOVA | 45 | 34 | 16 | 4 | 1 | 0 |
| alliance | 39 | 53 | 6 | 0 | 0 | 2 |
| c. give their staffs authority to make routine decisions on their own | | | | | | |
| total | 66 | 23 | 3 | 0 | 8 | * |
| GEO | 62 | 23 | 2 | 0 | 13 | 0 |
| ARNOVA | 75 | 17 | 4 | 0 | 3 | 1 |
| alliance | 61 | 29 | 2 | 0 | 7 | 0 |
| d. have few barriers between organization units—that is, staff from different parts of the organization are free to work together | | | | | | |
| total | 54 | 29 | 8 | 0 | 9 | * |
| GEO | 52 | 29 | 5 | 0 | 14 | 0 |
| ARNOVA | 57 | 27 | 12 | 0 | 4 | 0 |
| alliance | 52 | 30 | 8 | 0 | 8 | 1 |
| e. have a "rainy day" or reserve fund | | | | | | |
| total | 30 | 33 | 21 | 2 | 13 | * |
| GEO | 21 | 39 | 26 | 1 | 11 | 1 |
| ARNOVA | 36 | 25 | 18 | 4 | 17 | 0 |
| alliance | 34 | 34 | 18 | 2 | 12 | 0 |
| f. encourage staff to work in teams | | | | | | |
| total | 55 | 30 | 5 | * | 9 | * |
| GEO | 55 | 26 | 2 | 0 | 17 | 0 |
| ARNOVA | 58 | 30 | 5 | 1 | 5 | 0 |
| alliance | 53 | 35 | 6 | 0 | 5 | 1 |
| g. use information technology such as e-mail and the Internet to enhance performance | | | | | | |
| total | 74 | 21 | 3 | * | 1 | 0 |
| GEO | 67 | 27 | 6 | 0 | 0 | 0 |
| ARNOVA | 71 | 22 | 3 | 1 | 3 | 0 |
| alliance | 83 | 14 | 1 | 0 | 1 | 0 |

Q17.   How many of the high-performing organizations you know well have trouble retaining (Insert)—most, some, only a few, or none?

Based on those who know at least a few high-performing organizations,

Total n = 244, GEO n = 84, ARNOVA n = 77, alliance n = 83.

|  | Most | Some | Only a few | None | Don't know | Refused |
|---|---|---|---|---|---|---|
| a. staff | | | | | | |
| total | 23 | 45 | 25 | 6 | * | 0 |
| GEO | 25 | 46 | 25 | 4 | 0 | 0 |
| ARNOVA | 21 | 44 | 23 | 10 | 1 | 0 |
| alliance | 24 | 46 | 27 | 4 | 0 | 0 |
| b. leaders | | | | | | |
| total | 12 | 39 | 34 | 13 | 2 | 0 |
| GEO | 10 | 40 | 35 | 12 | 4 | 0 |
| ARNOVA | 19 | 35 | 27 | 16 | 3 | 0 |
| alliance | 8 | 40 | 40 | 12 | 0 | 0 |
| c. board members | | | | | | |
| total | 6 | 40 | 34 | 12 | 7 | 0 |
| GEO | 6 | 39 | 39 | 8 | 7 | 0 |
| ARNOVA | 8 | 35 | 30 | 18 | 9 | 0 |
| alliance | 5 | 45 | 34 | 11 | 6 | 0 |
| d. volunteers | | | | | | |
| total | 18 | 39 | 24 | 11 | 9 | * |
| GEO | 19 | 42 | 19 | 8 | 12 | 0 |
| ARNOVA | 19 | 29 | 27 | 14 | 10 | 0 |
| alliance | 16 | 45 | 25 | 10 | 4 | 1 |

Q18.   How many of the high-performing organizations you know well have experienced significant (Insert) in the past five years—most, some, only a few, or none?

Based on those who know at least a few high-performing organizations,

Total n = 244, GEO n = 84, ARNOVA n = 77, alliance n = 83.

| | Most | Some | Only a few | None | Don't know | Refused |
|---|---|---|---|---|---|---|
| a. rapid or moderate growth | | | | | | |
| total | 41 | 38 | 19 | 2 | * | 0 |
| GEO | 45 | 39 | 15 | 0 | 0 | 0 |
| ARNOVA | 35 | 38 | 22 | 4 | 1 | 0 |
| alliance | 41 | 37 | 19 | 2 | 0 | 0 |
| b. stability, but no real growth | | | | | | |
| total | 11 | 36 | 38 | 12 | 2 | 0 |
| GEO | 7 | 40 | 39 | 12 | 1 | 0 |
| ARNOVA | 10 | 30 | 35 | 22 | 3 | 0 |
| alliance | 16 | 39 | 39 | 4 | 4 | 0 |
| c. moderate or rapid decline | | | | | | |
| total | * | 5 | 32 | 61 | 2 | 0 |
| GEO | 0 | 6 | 30 | 64 | 0 | 0 |
| ARNOVA | 1 | 5 | 17 | 73 | 4 | 0 |
| alliance | 0 | 4 | 48 | 47 | 1 | 0 |

Q19.  And what's the *leadership* like of the high-performing organizations you know well? How many have executive directors (Insert)—most, some, only a few, or none?

Based on those who know at least a few high-performing organizations,

Total n = 244, GEO n = 84, ARNOVA n = 77, alliance n = 83.

| | Most | Some | Only a few | None | Don't know | Refused |
|---|---|---|---|---|---|---|
| a. who have a participatory style of management | | | | | | |
| total | 51 | 36 | 9 | 0 | 3 | 0 |
| GEO | 40 | 44 | 12 | 0 | 4 | 0 |
| ARNOVA | 61 | 26 | 12 | 0 | 1 | 0 |
| alliance | 52 | 39 | 5 | 0 | 5 | 0 |
| b. who are good fundraisers | | | | | | |
| total | 65 | 25 | 7 | 2 | 1 | 0 |
| GEO | 69 | 21 | 7 | 1 | 1 | 0 |
| ARNOVA | 56 | 30 | 9 | 4 | 1 | 0 |
| alliance | 69 | 24 | 6 | 0 | 1 | 0 |
| c. and boards that have a clear understanding of their respective roles | | | | | | |
| total | 59 | 28 | 9 | * | 4 | 0 |
| GEO | 61 | 29 | 7 | 0 | 4 | 0 |
| ARNOVA | 56 | 29 | 9 | 1 | 5 | 0 |
| alliance | 60 | 27 | 11 | 0 | 2 | 0 |
| d. who can be described as charismatic leaders | | | | | | |
| total | 32 | 48 | 18 | 2 | * | 0 |
| GEO | 30 | 49 | 20 | 1 | 0 | 0 |
| ARNOVA | 32 | 44 | 19 | 4 | 0 | 0 |
| alliance | 35 | 49 | 14 | 0 | 1 | 0 |
| e. who know how to motivate people | | | | | | |
| total | 70 | 24 | 5 | 0 | 1 | 0 |
| GEO | 74 | 19 | 6 | 0 | 1 | 0 |
| ARNOVA | 66 | 29 | 4 | 0 | 1 | 0 |
| alliance | 70 | 25 | 4 | 0 | 1 | 0 |
| f. who encourage risk taking | | | | | | |
| total | 41 | 41 | 11 | 1 | 6 | 0 |
| GEO | 42 | 35 | 14 | 1 | 8 | 0 |
| ARNOVA | 40 | 48 | 4 | 3 | 5 | 0 |
| alliance | 42 | 40 | 13 | 0 | 5 | 0 |
| g. who foster open communications | | | | | | |
| total | 72 | 23 | 4 | 0 | 2 | 0 |
| GEO | 76 | 18 | 4 | 0 | 2 | 0 |
| ARNOVA | 71 | 25 | 4 | 0 | 0 | 0 |
| alliance | 67 | 25 | 4 | 0 | 4 | 0 |

Q20.   How many of the high-performing organizations you know well have leaders (Insert)—most, some, only a few or none?

Based on those who know at least a few high-performing organizations,

Total n = 244, GEO n = 84, ARNOVA n = 77, alliance n = 83.

| | Most | Some | Only a few | None | Don't know | Refused |
|---|---|---|---|---|---|---|
| a. who have been in the nonprofit sector most of their career | | | | | | |
| total | 66 | 26 | 3 | * | 5 | 0 |
| GEO | 68 | 24 | 4 | 0 | 5 | 0 |
| ARNOVA | 53 | 35 | 5 | 1 | 5 | 0 |
| alliance | 75 | 20 | 1 | 0 | 4 | 0 |
| b. who have some experience in the private sector | | | | | | |
| total | 8 | 34 | 43 | 7 | 7 | 0 |
| GEO | 6 | 31 | 46 | 5 | 12 | 0 |
| ARNOVA | 9 | 38 | 34 | 13 | 6 | 0 |
| alliance | 8 | 35 | 49 | 5 | 2 | 0 |
| c. who have a graduate degree or advanced training in management | | | | | | |
| total | 22 | 25 | 36 | 9 | 9 | 0 |
| GEO | 12 | 24 | 43 | 7 | 14 | 0 |
| ARNOVA | 27 | 23 | 23 | 16 | 10 | 0 |
| alliance | 27 | 27 | 40 | 4 | 4 | 0 |
| d. who have been in their position less than five years | | | | | | |
| total | 10 | 47 | 32 | 9 | 3 | 0 |
| GEO | 13 | 46 | 29 | 7 | 5 | 0 |
| ARNOVA | 14 | 42 | 29 | 12 | 4 | 0 |
| alliance | 4 | 52 | 37 | 7 | 0 | 0 |
| e. are the founding director of the nonprofit organization itself | | | | | | |
| total | 5 | 26 | 50 | 18 | 1 | 0 |
| GEO | 7 | 36 | 45 | 11 | 1 | 0 |
| ARNOVA | 4 | 18 | 39 | 36 | 3 | 0 |
| alliance | 2 | 24 | 64 | 10 | 0 | 0 |

Q21.    What are the *internal management systems* like of the high-performing organizations you know well? How many (Insert)—most, some, only a few, or none?

Based on those who know at least a few high-performing organizations,

Total n = 244, GEO n = 84, ARNOVA n = 77, alliance n = 83.

| | Most | Some | Only a few | None | Don't know | Refused |
|---|---|---|---|---|---|---|
| **a. link staff pay to performance** | | | | | | |
| total | 15 | 30 | 31 | 10 | 14 | 0 |
| GEO | 13 | 29 | 30 | 10 | 19 | 0 |
| ARNOVA | 12 | 29 | 36 | 13 | 10 | 0 |
| alliance | 19 | 33 | 28 | 8 | 12 | 0 |
| **b. have position descriptions for their staff** | | | | | | |
| total | 77 | 14 | 3 | 0 | 6 | 0 |
| GEO | 74 | 12 | 4 | 0 | 11 | 0 |
| ARNOVA | 79 | 14 | 3 | 0 | 4 | 0 |
| alliance | 80 | 14 | 4 | 0 | 2 | 0 |
| **c. have an accurate, fast accounting system** | | | | | | |
| total | 47 | 31 | 8 | 0 | 14 | 0 |
| GEO | 49 | 27 | 7 | 0 | 17 | 0 |
| ARNOVA | 40 | 34 | 12 | 0 | 14 | 0 |
| alliance | 52 | 31 | 6 | 0 | 11 | 0 |
| **d. have programs or resources for staff training** | | | | | | |
| total | 52 | 29 | 14 | * | 4 | 0 |
| GEO | 33 | 38 | 20 | 0 | 8 | 0 |
| ARNOVA | 65 | 19 | 13 | 1 | 1 | 0 |
| alliance | 59 | 29 | 10 | 0 | 2 | 0 |
| **e. hold regular board meetings (at least 4 times a year)** | | | | | | |
| total | 90 | 4 | 3 | * | 2 | 0 |
| GEO | 95 | 2 | 0 | 0 | 2 | 0 |
| ARNOVA | 83 | 6 | 4 | 1 | 5 | 0 |
| alliance | 92 | 4 | 5 | 0 | 0 | 0 |
| **f. have adequate information technology** | | | | | | |
| total | 36 | 41 | 19 | 4 | * | 0 |
| GEO | 31 | 48 | 21 | 0 | 0 | 0 |
| ARNOVA | 39 | 31 | 22 | 8 | 0 | 0 |
| alliance | 39 | 43 | 13 | 4 | 1 | 0 |
| **g. have a strategic plan for the future** | | | | | | |
| total | 73 | 20 | 6 | * | 1 | 0 |
| GEO | 74 | 23 | 2 | 0 | 1 | 0 |
| ARNOVA | 68 | 21 | 10 | 0 | 1 | 0 |
| alliance | 76 | 17 | 5 | 1 | 1 | 0 |

*(continued)*

Q21.    What are the *internal management systems* like of the high-performing organizations you know well? How many (Insert)—most, some, only a few, or none? *(Continued)*

Based on those who know at least a few high-performing organizations,

Total n = 244, GEO n = 84, ARNOVA n = 77, alliance n = 83.

| | Most | Some | Only a few | None | Don't know | Refused |
|---|---|---|---|---|---|---|
| h. use data to make informed decisions | | | | | | |
| total | 63 | 25 | 7 | * | 5 | 0 |
| GEO | 57 | 30 | 6 | 0 | 7 | 0 |
| ARNOVA | 70 | 18 | 8 | 0 | 4 | 0 |
| alliance | 61 | 25 | 7 | 1 | 5 | 0 |

Q22.    Now thinking about these four aspects of an organization—its external relationships, internal organizational structure, leadership, and internal management systems—which is the most important one for a below-average-performing organization to improve first?

| total | GEO | ARNOVA | alliance | |
|---|---|---|---|---|
| 2 | 1 | 5 | 0 | External relationships |
| 14 | 18 | 16 | 10 | Internal organizational structure |
| 64 | 61 | 61 | 70 | Leadership |
| 17 | 18 | 18 | 16 | Internal management systems |
| 2 | 2 | 0 | 2 | Don't know |
| 1 | 0 | 0 | 2 | Refused |
| 244 | 84 | 77 | 83 | Based on those who know at least a few high-performing organizations or are familiar with literature on organizational performance |

Q23a.   Which of the following components of an organization's external
relationships is most important to improve first? Is it most important to
... (Read)

| total | GEO | ARNOVA | alliance | |
|---|---|---|---|---|
| 20 | 0 | 25 | 0 | Collaborate with other organizations |
| 40 | 100 | 25 | 0 | Have a diversified funding base |
| 0 | 0 | 0 | 0 | Rely on volunteers to deliver at least some of their services |
| 20 | 0 | 25 | 0 | Regularly survey clients regarding programs and services |
| 0 | 0 | 0 | 0 | Measure the results or outcomes of what they do |
| 20 | 0 | 25 | 0 | Generate at least some unrestricted revenue |
| 0 | 0 | 0 | 0 | Other (Volunteered) |
| 0 | 0 | 0 | 0 | None (Volunteered) |
| 0 | 0 | 0 | 0 | Don't know |
| 0 | 0 | 0 | 0 | Refused |
| 5 | 1 | 4 | 0 | Based on those who believe external relationships should be improved first |

Q23b.   Which of the following components of an organization's internal
organizational structure is most important to improve first? Is it most
important to ... (Read)

| total | GEO | ARNOVA | alliance | |
|---|---|---|---|---|
| 14 | 13 | 25 | 0 | Have few layers of management between the top and bottom of the organization |
| 0 | 0 | 0 | 0 | Have demographically diverse staffs |
| 23 | 27 | 17 | 25 | Give staff authority to make routine decisions on their own |
| 20 | 13 | 33 | 13 | Have few barriers between organizational units |
| 3 | 7 | 0 | 0 | Have a "rainy day" or reserve fund |
| 29 | 27 | 17 | 50 | Encourage staff to work in teams |
| 6 | 0 | 8 | 13 | Use information technology to enhance performance |
| 3 | 7 | 0 | 0 | Other (Volunteered) |
| 0 | 0 | 0 | 0 | None (Volunteered) |
| 3 | 7 | 0 | 0 | Don't know |
| 0 | 0 | 0 | 0 | Refused |
| 35 | 15 | 12 | 8 | Based on those who believe internal organizational structure should be improved first |

Q23c.   Which of the following components of an organization's leadership is most important to improve first? Is it most important for leaders to . . . (Read)

| total | GEO | ARNOVA | alliance | |
|---|---|---|---|---|
| 17 | 20 | 13 | 17 | Have a participatory style of management |
| 3 | 4 | 2 | 3 | Fundraise |
| 31 | 43 | 30 | 21 | Have a clear understanding with their boards about their respective roles |
| 3 | 2 | 4 | 2 | Be charismatic |
| 20 | 16 | 26 | 19 | Know how to motivate people |
| 3 | 2 | 2 | 5 | Encourage risk taking |
| 11 | 4 | 11 | 17 | Foster open communication |
| 6 | 6 | 2 | 9 | Other (Volunteered) |
| 1 | 2 | 0 | 2 | None (Volunteered) |
| 3 | 0 | 9 | 0 | Don't know |
| 3 | 2 | 2 | 5 | Refused |
| 156 | 51 | 47 | 58 | Based on those who believe leadership should be improved first |

Q23d.   Which of the following components of an organization's internal management systems should be improved first? Is it most important to . . . (Read)

| total | GEO | ARNOVA | alliance | |
|---|---|---|---|---|
| 5 | 7 | 7 | 0 | Link staff pay to performance |
| 5 | 0 | 14 | 0 | Have position descriptions for their staff |
| 7 | 13 | 7 | 0 | Have an accurate, fast accounting system |
| 10 | 20 | 0 | 8 | Have programs or resources for staff training |
| 2 | 0 | 7 | 0 | Hold regular board meetings (at least 4 times a year) |
| 2 | 0 | 7 | 0 | Have adequate information technology |
| 52 | 47 | 43 | 69 | Have a strategic plan for the future |
| 17 | 13 | 14 | 23 | Use data to make informed decisions |
| 0 | 0 | 0 | 0 | Other (Volunteered) |
| 0 | 0 | 0 | 0 | None (Volunteered) |
| 0 | 0 | 0 | 0 | Don't know |
| 0 | 0 | 0 | 0 | Refused |
| 42 | 15 | 14 | 13 | Based on those who believe internal management systems should be improved first |

Q24.   A variety of organizations are trying to improve nonprofit performance. In your opinion, how much do(es) (Insert) contribute to improving nonprofit performance—a great deal, a fair amount, not too much, or nothing at all?

| | A great deal | A fair amount | Not too much | Nothing at all | Don't know | Refused |
|---|---|---|---|---|---|---|
| a. foundations | | | | | | |
| total | 8 | 34 | 53 | 3 | 2 | * |
| GEO | 6 | 39 | 49 | 2 | 2 | 1 |
| ARNOVA | 10 | 40 | 48 | 0 | 3 | 0 |
| alliance | 8 | 24 | 61 | 6 | 1 | 0 |
| b. the government | | | | | | |
| total | 1 | 13 | 54 | 28 | 3 | * |
| GEO | 0 | 5 | 58 | 33 | 5 | 0 |
| ARNOVA | 1 | 26 | 50 | 20 | 1 | 1 |
| alliance | 2 | 9 | 54 | 32 | 2 | 0 |
| c. graduate schools that train nonprofit executives and staff | | | | | | |
| total | 16 | 44 | 31 | 3 | 7 | 0 |
| GEO | 9 | 47 | 34 | 2 | 7 | 0 |
| ARNOVA | 26 | 41 | 25 | 4 | 4 | 0 |
| alliance | 12 | 42 | 33 | 4 | 9 | 0 |
| d. management service organziations | | | | | | |
| total | 25 | 46 | 20 | 2 | 6 | 1 |
| GEO | 18 | 52 | 21 | 1 | 8 | 0 |
| ARNOVA | 16 | 40 | 33 | 3 | 9 | 0 |
| alliance | 41 | 45 | 8 | 2 | 1 | 2 |
| e. external rating organizations | | | | | | |
| total | 2 | 16 | 43 | 19 | 20 | 0 |
| GEO | 2 | 7 | 46 | 24 | 21 | 0 |
| ARNOVA | 1 | 23 | 39 | 20 | 18 | 0 |
| alliance | 2 | 20 | 45 | 13 | 20 | 0 |
| f. providers of technical assistance | | | | | | |
| total | 30 | 54 | 11 | 2 | 2 | 0 |
| GEO | 28 | 61 | 8 | 0 | 2 | 0 |
| ARNOVA | 19 | 54 | 18 | 5 | 5 | 0 |
| alliance | 44 | 47 | 8 | 1 | 0 | 0 |
| g. associations of nonprofits | | | | | | |
| total | 20 | 54 | 21 | 2 | 3 | 0 |
| GEO | 16 | 54 | 24 | 1 | 5 | 0 |
| ARNOVA | 26 | 50 | 19 | 1 | 4 | 0 |
| alliance | 18 | 58 | 20 | 4 | 1 | 0 |

Q25.    In your opinion, what one change would make the biggest difference in improving nonprofit performance?

| total | GEO | ARNOVA | alliance | |
|---|---|---|---|---|
| 96 | 95 | 95 | 99 | Gave Response |
| 3 | 5 | 4 | 1 | Don't know |
| * | 0 | 1 | 0 | Refused |

Q26.    There have been a number of proposals over the past few years to improve nonprofit performance. Has (Insert) improved performance a great deal, a fair amount, not too much, or not at all?

| | A great deal | A fair amount | Not too much | Nothing at all | Don't know | Refused |
|---|---|---|---|---|---|---|
| a. the creation of management standards | | | | | | |
| total | 13 | 39 | 30 | 8 | 10 | * |
| GEO | 16 | 27 | 36 | 4 | 16 | 0 |
| ARNOVA | 9 | 49 | 25 | 10 | 8 | 0 |
| alliance | 13 | 42 | 28 | 11 | 5 | 1 |
| b. the encouragement to collaborate with other nonprofits | | | | | | |
| total | 17 | 44 | 30 | 5 | 2 | * |
| GEO | 18 | 42 | 36 | 2 | 1 | 0 |
| ARNOVA | 24 | 44 | 23 | 5 | 5 | 0 |
| alliance | 11 | 47 | 32 | 8 | 1 | 1 |
| c. making nonprofits more open to the public and media | | | | | | |
| total | 13 | 35 | 39 | 7 | 5 | * |
| GEO | 11 | 35 | 44 | 6 | 5 | 0 |
| ARNOVA | 19 | 46 | 24 | 8 | 4 | 0 |
| alliance | 11 | 25 | 48 | 8 | 7 | 1 |
| d. reducing duplication and overlap among nonprofits through mergers and alliances | | | | | | |
| total | 12 | 39 | 36 | 6 | 6 | * |
| GEO | 12 | 42 | 33 | 5 | 8 | 0 |
| ARNOVA | 14 | 31 | 39 | 9 | 8 | 0 |
| alliance | 12 | 42 | 38 | 5 | 2 | 1 |
| e. strengthening external reviews by the Better Business Bureau, GuideStar, and the National Charities Information Bureau | | | | | | |
| total | 4 | 16 | 48 | 19 | 12 | * |
| GEO | 1 | 13 | 51 | 21 | 14 | 0 |
| ARNOVA | 13 | 18 | 38 | 15 | 18 | 0 |
| alliance | 0 | 18 | 55 | 21 | 5 | 1 |

(continued)

Q26.    There have been a number of proposals over the past few years to improve nonprofit performance. Has (Insert) improved performance a great deal, a fair amount, not too much, or not at all? *(Continued)*

| | A great deal | A fair amount | Not too much | Nothing at all | Don't know | Refused |
|---|---|---|---|---|---|---|
| **f.  the encouragement to do more strategic planning** | | | | | | |
| total | 41 | 46 | 10 | * | 2 | * |
| GEO | 41 | 51 | 6 | 0 | 2 | 0 |
| ARNOVA | 36 | 49 | 11 | 0 | 4 | 0 |
| alliance | 46 | 39 | 13 | 1 | 0 | 1 |
| **g.  giving executive directors greater accesss to training in running organizations** | | | | | | |
| total | 40 | 48 | 8 | * | 4 | * |
| GEO | 51 | 35 | 8 | 0 | 6 | 0 |
| ARNOVA | 38 | 50 | 8 | 1 | 4 | 0 |
| alliance | 32 | 58 | 7 | 0 | 2 | 1 |
| **h.  encouraging executive directors to stay for longer periods in their jobs** | | | | | | |
| total | 15 | 35 | 27 | 7 | 14 | 1 |
| GEO | 11 | 35 | 29 | 6 | 19 | 0 |
| ARNOVA | 21 | 40 | 18 | 8 | 13 | 1 |
| alliance | 14 | 31 | 33 | 8 | 12 | 2 |
| **i.  encouraging foundations to provide more funding for capacity building** | | | | | | |
| total | 38 | 42 | 14 | * | 5 | * |
| GEO | 33 | 49 | 11 | 0 | 7 | 0 |
| ARNOVA | 36 | 36 | 18 | 1 | 9 | 0 |
| alliance | 44 | 40 | 15 | 0 | 0 | 1 |
| **j.  an increased emphasis on outcomes measurement** | | | | | | |
| total | 22 | 44 | 27 | 4 | 2 | * |
| GEO | 24 | 46 | 26 | 2 | 2 | 0 |
| ARNOVA | 18 | 50 | 25 | 5 | 3 | 0 |
| alliance | 25 | 38 | 31 | 5 | 1 | 1 |
| **k.  management assistance grants** | | | | | | |
| total | 28 | 49 | 9 | 1 | 12 | * |
| GEO | 31 | 55 | 7 | 0 | 7 | 0 |
| ARNOVA | 19 | 44 | 14 | 1 | 23 | 0 |
| alliance | 35 | 47 | 7 | 2 | 7 | 1 |
| **l.  increased openness to using standard business tools or techniques** | | | | | | |
| total | 24 | 53 | 15 | 4 | 4 | * |
| GEO | 22 | 51 | 20 | 1 | 6 | 0 |
| ARNOVA | 30 | 49 | 10 | 6 | 5 | 0 |
| alliance | 20 | 59 | 15 | 4 | 1 | 1 |
| **m. more active donor involvement or oversight** | | | | | | |
| total | 8 | 31 | 40 | 14 | 7 | * |
| GEO | 7 | 26 | 47 | 9 | 11 | 0 |
| ARNOVA | 11 | 34 | 36 | 11 | 8 | 0 |
| alliance | 5 | 34 | 35 | 22 | 2 | 1 |

D1.   Sex

| total | GEO | ARNOVA | alliance | |
|---|---|---|---|---|
| 34 | 31 | 44 | 29 | Male |
| 66 | 69 | 56 | 71 | Female |

D2.   What is your age?[1]

| total | GEO | ARNOVA | alliance | |
|---|---|---|---|---|
| 3 | 5 | 4 | 1 | 18–29 |
| 20 | 22 | 21 | 18 | 30–39 |
| 35 | 35 | 34 | 35 | 40–49 |
| 32 | 31 | 29 | 38 | 50–59 |
| 7 | 5 | 10 | 7 | 60–69 |
| 0 | 0 | 0 | 0 | 70 or older |
| 0 | 0 | 0 | 0 | Don't know |
| 2 | 2 | 3 | 1 | Refused |

1. Based on those who gave a numeric response.

D3.   In general, would you describe your political views as very conservative, conservative, moderate, liberal, or very liberal?

| total | GEO | ARNOVA | alliance | |
|---|---|---|---|---|
| * | 0 | 1 | 0 | Very conservative |
| 3 | 4 | 5 | 0 | Conservative |
| 29 | 22 | 34 | 32 | Moderate |
| 42 | 52 | 36 | 39 | Liberal |
| 22 | 16 | 23 | 28 | Very liberal |
| * | 0 | 1 | 0 | Don't know |
| 2 | 6 | 0 | 1 | Refused |

D4.   Which of these best describes your race and ethnicity? White, black or African American, Hispanic or Latino, Asian, or something else?

| total | GEO | ARNOVA | alliance | |
|---|---|---|---|---|
| 87 | 89 | 89 | 84 | White |
| 6 | 6 | 4 | 7 | Black or African-American |
| 3 | 2 | 3 | 4 | Hispanic or Latino |
| 3 | 1 | 4 | 4 | Asian |
| * | 0 | 1 | 0 | Other |
| 0 | 0 | 0 | 0 | Don't know |
| 1 | 1 | 0 | 2 | Refused |

# Executive Directors' Survey

N = 250 executives of high-performing nonprofits

Margin of error ±6% for sample

Q1.  What is your position in the organization?[1,2]

| All | Small | Medium | Large | |
|-----|-------|--------|-------|--|
| 72 | 76 | 80 | 55 | President/CaO/executive director |
| 4 | 1 | 6 | 5 | COO/CFO/Associate executive director |
| 6 | 1 | 3 | 16 | Vice president |
| 12 | 17 | 8 | 12 | Director/co-director/manager |
| 2 | 0 | 3 | 2 | Assistant director/executive assistant |
| 4 | 6 | 0 | 10 | Other |
| 0 | 0 | 0 | 0 | Don't know |
| 0 | 0 | 0 | 0 | Refused |

Q2.  How many years have you been with the organization?

| All | Small | Medium | Large | |
|-----|-------|--------|-------|--|
| 26 | 29 | 19 | 33 | Less than 5 years |
| 45 | 54 | 46 | 28 | 5–14 years |
| 29 | 17 | 35 | 40 | 15 years or more |
| 0 | 0 | 0 | 0 | Don't know |
| 0 | 0 | 0 | 0 | Refused |

1. Because results are rounded they may not total exactly 100%.
2. 'All' refers to all people answering the survey. 'Small' refers to those in organizations with less than a million dollar annual budget. 'Medium' refers to those in organizations with an annual budget between two and ten million dollars. 'Large' refers to those in organizations with an annual budget greater than ten million dollars.

Q3.  And what is your organization's primary focus—is it . . .

Multiple responses were accepted

| All | Small | Medium | Large | |
|-----|-------|--------|-------|---|
| 6 | 11 | 3 | 5 | The arts and culture |
| 6 | 8 | 4 | 7 | The environment/agriculture |
| 26 | 33 | 24 | 17 | Community development/housing/ homelessness |
| 19 | 11 | 24 | 22 | Nutrition or hunger/human services |
| 14 | 14 | 12 | 16 | Education/job training |
| 14 | 7 | 16 | 22 | Children and youth |
| 11 | 10 | 9 | 17 | Health/HIV/drugs |
| 33 | 29 | 38 | 31 | Other |
| 0 | 0 | 0 | 0 | Don't know |
| 0 | 0 | 0 | 0 | Refused |

Q4.  How long has your organization been in operation—less than 7 years, 7 to 15 years, 16 to 30 years, or more than 30 years?

| All | Small | Medium | Large | |
|-----|-------|--------|-------|---|
| 8 | 16 | 5 | 2 | Less than 7 years |
| 20 | 36 | 14 | 5 | 7 to 15 years |
| 30 | 31 | 39 | 14 | 16 to 30 years |
| 42 | 18 | 42 | 79 | More than 30 years |
| 0 | 0 | 0 | 0 | Don't know |
| 0 | 0 | 0 | 0 | Refused |

Q5.  Roughly, how many employees work for your organization?

| All | Small | Medium | Large | |
|-----|-------|--------|-------|---|
| 25 | 62 | 6 | 0 | Less than 15 |
| 15 | 21 | 17 | 0 | 15–29 |
| 14 | 10 | 23 | 3 | 30–49 |
| 46 | 7 | 54 | 95 | 50 or more |
| * | 0 | 0 | 2 | Don't know |
| 0 | 0 | 0 | 0 | Refused |

Q6.  Roughly, how many volunteers work for your organization?

| All | Small | Medium | Large | |
|-----|-------|--------|-------|---|
| 26 | 31 | 32 | 5 | Less than 30 |
| 38 | 47 | 35 | 31 | 30–299 |
| 32 | 21 | 31 | 53 | 300 or more |
| 3 | 1 | 1 | 9 | Don't know |
| 1 | 0 | 1 | 2 | Refused |

Q7.  Which of these categories best describes the size of your organization's budget? Is it . . .

| All | Small | Medium | Large | |
|---|---|---|---|---|
| 12 | 32 | 0 | 0 | Less than $500,000 annual budget |
| 24 | 68 | 0 | 0 | $500,000 to a million |
| 40 | 0 | 100 | 0 | Two million to $10 million |
| 23 | 0 | 0 | 100 | More than $10 million |
| 1 | 0 | 0 | 0 | Don't know |
| 0 | 0 | 0 | 0 | Refused |

Q8.  Is your organization a national headquarters, a local chapter, or an independent nonprofit?

| All | Small | Medium | Large | |
|---|---|---|---|---|
| 9 | 6 | 5 | 21 | National headquarters |
| 8 | 4 | 11 | 7 | Local chapter |
| 82 | 89 | 83 | 72 | Independent |
| 1 | 1 | 1 | 0 | Don't know |
| 0 | 0 | 0 | 0 | Refused |

Q9.  How much of your professional career have you spent in the nonprofit sector? Have you spent all of your career, most, half, or less than half of your professional career in the nonprofit sector?

| All | Small | Medium | Large | |
|---|---|---|---|---|
| 43 | 31 | 54 | 45 | All of your career |
| 32 | 40 | 29 | 22 | Most |
| 10 | 13 | 6 | 12 | Half |
| 15 | 16 | 11 | 21 | Less than half |
| 0 | 0 | 0 | 0 | Don't know |
| 0 | 0 | 0 | 0 | Refused |

Q10.  And how much of your professional career have you spent in the private sector—all of your career, most, half, or less than half of your career in the private sector?

| All | Small | Medium | Large | |
|---|---|---|---|---|
| 8 | 13 | 6 | 2 | All of your career |
| 10 | 8 | 8 | 17 | Most |
| 11 | 17 | 3 | 14 | Half |
| 68 | 60 | 81 | 62 | Less than half |
| 3 | 2 | 1 | 5 | Don't know |
| * | 0 | 1 | 0 | Refused |

Q11.  Is the founding director of your organization still running the organization or not?

| All | Small | Medium | Large | |
|---|---|---|---|---|
| 41 | 49 | 31 | 42 | Yes |
| 59 | 51 | 69 | 58 | No |
| 0 | 0 | 0 | 0 | Don't know |
| 0 | 0 | 0 | 0 | Refused |
| $n = 145$ | $n = 74$ | $n = 58$ | $n = 12$ | Based on those whose organization is 30 years old or less. |

Q12.  Words often have somewhat different meanings to different people. When you hear the phrase "organizational effectiveness" what does it mean to you?

| All | Small | Medium | Large | |
|---|---|---|---|---|
| 100 | 100 | 100 | 100 | Gave response |
| 0 | 0 | 0 | 0 | Don't know |
| 0 | 0 | 0 | 0 | Refused |

Q13.  Now I'm going to read you 6 words that could describe a high-performing nonprofit organization. The 6 words are (Insert all 6 words). In your opinion, which of these 6 words is the most important characteristic of a high-performing nonprofit organization? Again the 6 words are (Insert all 6 words).

| All | Small | Medium | Large | |
|---|---|---|---|---|
| 4 | 4 | 3 | 3 | Rigorous |
| 26 | 28 | 27 | 21 | Innovative |
| 18 | 18 | 17 | 19 | Collaborative |
| 23 | 23 | 20 | 28 | Principled |
| 10 | 9 | 10 | 10 | Resilient |
| 19 | 17 | 21 | 17 | Entrepreneurial |
| 1 | 0 | 2 | 0 | Don't know |
| 1 | 1 | 0 | 2 | Refused |

Q14.   In your opinion, how important is it for a leader of a high-performing nonprofit organization to be (Insert). Is it very important, somewhat important, not too important, or not important at all?

| | Very important | Somewhat important | Not too important | Not important at all | Don't know | Refused |
|---|---|---|---|---|---|---|
| a. Decisive | | | | | | |
| Total | 79 | 21 | 0 | 0 | 0 | 0 |
| Small | 72 | 28 | 0 | 0 | 0 | 0 |
| Medium | 77 | 23 | 0 | 0 | 0 | 0 |
| Large | 93 | 7 | 0 | 0 | 0 | 0 |
| b. Honest | | | | | | |
| Total | 98 | 2 | 0 | * | 0 | 0 |
| Small | 97 | 2 | 0 | 1 | 0 | 0 |
| Medium | 97 | 3 | 0 | 0 | 0 | 0 |
| Large | 100 | 0 | 0 | 0 | 0 | 0 |
| c. Charismatic | | | | | | |
| Total | 35 | 60 | 4 | 1 | 0 | 0 |
| Small | 46 | 51 | 3 | 0 | 0 | 0 |
| Medium | 32 | 62 | 5 | 1 | 0 | 0 |
| Large | 26 | 69 | 3 | 2 | 0 | 0 |
| d. Faithful | | | | | | |
| Total | 85 | 10 | 1 | * | 2 | 1 |
| Small | 89 | 9 | 0 | 0 | 2 | 0 |
| Medium | 80 | 12 | 1 | 1 | 4 | 2 |
| Large | 88 | 7 | 3 | 0 | 0 | 2 |
| e. Trusting | | | | | | |
| Total | 75 | 22 | 2 | 0 | 0 | * |
| Small | 74 | 22 | 2 | 0 | 0 | 1 |
| Medium | 75 | 23 | 2 | 0 | 0 | 0 |
| Large | 74 | 22 | 3 | 0 | 0 | 0 |

Q15.   Now I'm going to read you the characteristics you said were very important for leaders of a high-performing organization (Insert all very important responses). Which of these is the most important characteristic of a leader of a high-performing nonprofit organization?

| All | Small | Medium | Large | |
|---|---|---|---|---|
| 19 | 25 | 14 | 14 | Decisive |
| 47 | 37 | 51 | 56 | Honest |
| 5 | 4 | 8 | 2 | Charismatic |
| 14 | 16 | 13 | 12 | Faithful |
| 13 | 15 | 12 | 11 | Trusting |
| 3 | 3 | 2 | 4 | Don't know |
| * | 0 | 0 | 2 | Refused |
| $n = 248$ | $n = 89$ | $n = 100$ | $n = 57$ | Based on those who choose more than one issue as 'very important.' |

Q16.   And in your opinion, how important is it that a leader of a high-performing nonprofit organization (Insert). Is it very important, somewhat important, not too important, or not important at all?

| | Very important | Somewhat important | Not too important | Not important at all | Don't know | Refused |
|---|---|---|---|---|---|---|
| a. Be a good fundraiser | | | | | | |
| Total | 72 | 26 | 1 | 1 | 0 | 0 |
| Small | 71 | 29 | 0 | 0 | 0 | 0 |
| Medium | 77 | 21 | 1 | 1 | 0 | 0 |
| Large | 67 | 28 | 3 | 2 | 0 | 0 |
| b. Encourages risk-taking | | | | | | |
| Total | 66 | 33 | 1 | 0 | 0 | 0 |
| Small | 58 | 40 | 2 | 0 | 0 | 0 |
| Medium | 75 | 25 | 0 | 0 | 0 | 0 |
| Large | 64 | 36 | 0 | 0 | 0 | 0 |
| c. Knows how to motivate people | | | | | | |
| Total | 92 | 8 | 0 | 0 | * | 0 |
| Small | 93 | 7 | 0 | 0 | 0 | 0 |
| Medium | 93 | 6 | 0 | 0 | 1 | 0 |
| Large | 86 | 14 | 0 | 0 | 0 | 0 |

Q17.    Please tell me if you strongly agree, somewhat agree, somewhat disagree or strongly disagree with these statements.

|  | Strongly agree | Somewhat agree | Somewhat disagree | Strongly disagree | Don't know | Refused |
|---|---|---|---|---|---|---|
| a. An organization can be very well managed and still not achieve its program goals | | | | | | |
| Total | 35 | 41 | 13 | 11 | 0 | 0 |
| Small | 34 | 47 | 12 | 7 | 0 | 0 |
| Medium | 35 | 40 | 15 | 10 | 0 | 0 |
| Large | 36 | 33 | 12 | 19 | 0 | 0 |
| b. An organization can be very effective in achieving its program goals but not be well managed | | | | | | |
| Total | 16 | 32 | 33 | 20 | * | 0 |
| Small | 13 | 36 | 33 | 17 | 1 | 0 |
| Medium | 19 | 31 | 29 | 21 | 0 | 0 |
| Large | 14 | 26 | 38 | 22 | 0 | 0 |
| c. Most nonprofit organizations are better managed today than they were five years ago | | | | | | |
| Total | 34 | 46 | 6 | 1 | 12 | 0 |
| Small | 30 | 43 | 10 | 1 | 16 | 0 |
| Medium | 36 | 48 | 4 | 1 | 11 | 0 |
| Large | 36 | 50 | 5 | 0 | 9 | 0 |

Q18.    Based on your organization's experience, if you were advising another similar nonprofit on how to become a high-performing organization, would you tell them to first work on becoming well managed or to work on increasing their program impacts?

| All | Small | Medium | Large | |
|---|---|---|---|---|
| 59 | 60 | 64 | 48 | First work on becoming well managed |
| 31 | 26 | 29 | 45 | Work on increasing program impacts |
| 9 | 13 | 7 | 5 | Both |
| * | 1 | 0 | 0 | Don't know |
| * | 0 | 0 | 2 | Refused |

Q19.   Let's talk about how your organization deals with its external relationships, that is, the outside world. To what extent does your organization (Insert)—a large extent, a fair extent, not too much, or not at all?

| | A large extent | A fair extent | Not too much | Not at all | Don't know | Refused |
|---|---|---|---|---|---|---|
| **a. Collaborate with other organizations** | | | | | | |
| Total | 75 | 22 | 3 | 0 | 0 | 0 |
| Small | 76 | 21 | 3 | 0 | 0 | 0 |
| Medium | 78 | 21 | 1 | 0 | 0 | 0 |
| Large | 71 | 24 | 5 | 0 | 0 | 0 |
| **b. Have a diversified funding base** | | | | | | |
| Total | 56 | 35 | 6 | 2 | 1 | 0 |
| Small | 47 | 44 | 8 | 1 | 0 | 0 |
| Medium | 62 | 28 | 6 | 4 | 0 | 0 |
| Large | 59 | 34 | 5 | 0 | 2 | 0 |
| **c. Rely on volunteers to deliver at least some of your services** | | | | | | |
| Total | 40 | 22 | 27 | 10 | * | 0 |
| Small | 52 | 23 | 17 | 8 | 0 | 0 |
| Medium | 33 | 19 | 37 | 10 | 1 | 0 |
| Large | 33 | 26 | 26 | 16 | 0 | 0 |
| **d. Regularly survey your clients regarding programs and services** | | | | | | |
| Total | 54 | 38 | 6 | 2 | 1 | 0 |
| Small | 48 | 41 | 7 | 3 | 1 | 0 |
| Medium | 50 | 42 | 6 | 2 | 0 | 0 |
| Large | 71 | 22 | 5 | 0 | 2 | 0 |
| **e. Measure the results or outcomes of what you do** | | | | | | |
| Total | 64 | 31 | 4 | 1 | 0 | 0 |
| Small | 62 | 31 | 4 | 2 | 0 | 0 |
| Medium | 58 | 37 | 5 | 0 | 0 | 0 |
| Large | 76 | 22 | 2 | 0 | 0 | 0 |
| **f. Generate at least some unrestricted revenue** | | | | | | |
| Total | 53 | 33 | 11 | 2 | 1 | 0 |
| Small | 47 | 36 | 13 | 2 | 2 | 0 |
| Medium | 56 | 35 | 7 | 2 | 0 | 0 |
| Large | 59 | 28 | 14 | 0 | 0 | 0 |

Q20.    And to what extent has your organization experienced significant growth in demand for your programs and services over the past five years— a large extent, a fair extent, not too much, or not at all?

| All | Small | Medium | Large | |
|---|---|---|---|---|
| 79 | 86 | 76 | 72 | A large extent |
| 18 | 11 | 21 | 24 | A fair extent |
| 3 | 2 | 3 | 3 | Not too much |
| 0 | 0 | 0 | 0 | Not at all |
| * | 1 | 0 | 0 | Don't know |
| 0 | 0 | 0 | 0 | Refused |

Q21.    Does (Insert) describe the general environment of your organization very well, somewhat well, not too well, or not well at all?

| | Very well | Somewhat well | Not too well | Not well at all | Don't know | Refused |
|---|---|---|---|---|---|---|
| a. Turbulent | | | | | | |
| Total | 12 | 22 | 27 | 39 | 1 | 0 |
| Small | 10 | 18 | 22 | 48 | 2 | 0 |
| Medium | 9 | 20 | 31 | 40 | 0 | 0 |
| Large | 19 | 31 | 26 | 24 | 0 | 0 |
| b. Competitive | | | | | | |
| Total | 27 | 32 | 18 | 21 | 2 | 0 |
| Small | 22 | 21 | 20 | 33 | 3 | 0 |
| Medium | 25 | 39 | 19 | 15 | 2 | 0 |
| Large | 38 | 36 | 14 | 12 | 0 | 0 |
| c. Heavily regulated | | | | | | |
| Total | 15 | 23 | 27 | 34 | 1 | 0 |
| Small | 10 | 19 | 29 | 41 | 1 | 0 |
| Medium | 14 | 24 | 26 | 35 | 1 | 0 |
| Large | 24 | 24 | 26 | 24 | 2 | 0 |

Q22. Now I'd like to learn more about your *internal organizational structure.* How many layers of management does your organization have between the top and bottom of the organization?

| All | Small | Medium | Large | |
|---|---|---|---|---|
| 2 | 3 | 1 | 0 | Zero |
| 21 | 33 | 19 | 5 | One |
| 25 | 31 | 28 | 9 | Two |
| 27 | 27 | 25 | 33 | Three |
| 15 | 3 | 18 | 28 | Four |
| 6 | 1 | 5 | 16 | Five |
| 2 | 0 | 2 | 3 | Six |
| 1 | 0 | 1 | 2 | Seven |
| 2 | 1 | 1 | 3 | Don't know |
| * | 0 | 0 | 2 | Refused |

Q23. How demographically diverse is your staff? A very diverse staff is made up of young and old, male and female, black, Latino, and white staff members—is your organization's staff very diverse, somewhat diverse, not too diverse, or not diverse at all?

| All | Small | Medium | Large | |
|---|---|---|---|---|
| 51 | 42 | 55 | 59 | Very diverse |
| 39 | 42 | 38 | 36 | Somewhat diverse |
| 8 | 12 | 7 | 5 | Not too diverse |
| 1 | 3 | 0 | 0 | Not diverse at all |
| 0 | 0 | 0 | 0 | Don't know |
| 0 | 0 | 0 | 0 | Refused |

Q24. Which best describes how staff make routine decisions in your organization?

| All | Small | Medium | Large | |
|---|---|---|---|---|
| 79 | 73 | 82 | 83 | The staff make routine decisions on their own |
| 20 | 24 | 17 | 17 | The staff generally consult with the executive director or senior staff when making routine decisions |
| 1 | 2 | 0 | 0 | Don't know |
| * | 0 | 1 | 0 | Refused |

Q25.   Please tell me if you strongly agree, somewhat agree, somewhat disagree, or strongly disagree with these statements.

| | Strongly agree | Somewhat agree | Somewhat disagree | Strongly disagree | Don't know | Refused |
|---|---|---|---|---|---|---|
| a  Our organization uses information technology such as email and the Internet to enhance performance | | | | | | |
| Total | 80 | 18 | 2 | 1 | 0 | 0 |
| Small | 72 | 23 | 2 | 2 | 0 | 0 |
| Medium | 84 | 15 | 1 | 0 | 0 | 0 |
| Large | 84 | 14 | 2 | 0 | 0 | 0 |
| c  Staff from different parts of our organization rarely work together | | | | | | |
| Total | 3 | 7 | 15 | 75 | * | 0 |
| Small | 2 | 4 | 8 | 84 | 1 | 0 |
| Medium | 1 | 8 | 20 | 71 | 0 | 0 |
| Large | 7 | 7 | 17 | 69 | 0 | 0 |
| d  Our organization encourages staff to work in teams | | | | | | |
| Total | 82 | 17 | 1 | 0 | * | 0 |
| Small | 81 | 16 | 2 | 0 | 1 | 0 |
| Medium | 83 | 17 | 0 | 0 | 0 | 0 |
| Large | 81 | 19 | 0 | 0 | 0 | 0 |

Q26.   How much of a "rainy day" or reserve fund does your organization have—a large fund, a moderate fund, a small fund, or no fund at all?

| All | Small | Medium | Large | |
|---|---|---|---|---|
| 19 | 10 | 15 | 40 | A large fund |
| 41 | 42 | 45 | 33 | A moderate fund |
| 32 | 36 | 35 | 22 | A small fund |
| 7 | 11 | 4 | 5 | No fund at all |
| 1 | 1 | 0 | 0 | Don't know |
| * | 0 | 1 | 0 | Refused |

Q27.  How difficult has it been for your organization to retain (Insert)—
very difficult, somewhat difficult, not too difficult, or not difficult at all?

|  | Very difficult | Somewhat difficult | Not too difficult | Not difficult at all | Don't have board members | Don't know | Refused |
|---|---|---|---|---|---|---|---|
| a. Staff |  |  |  |  |  |  |  |
| Total | 3 | 38 | 33 | 25 | 1 | 0 | 0 |
| Small | 2 | 22 | 42 | 31 | 2 | 0 | 0 |
| Medium | 3 | 45 | 26 | 26 | 0 | 0 | 0 |
| Large | 3 | 53 | 29 | 14 | 0 | 0 | 0 |
| b. Leaders |  |  |  |  |  |  |  |
| Total | 2 | 19 | 34 | 44 | 0 | * | * |
| Small | 3 | 16 | 36 | 44 | 0 | 0 | 1 |
| Medium | 3 | 22 | 32 | 42 | 0 | 1 | 0 |
| Large | 0 | 19 | 34 | 47 | 0 | 0 | 0 |
| c. Board members |  |  |  |  |  |  |  |
| Total | 1 | 11 | 31 | 57 | * | 0 | 0 |
| Small | 1 | 16 | 38 | 44 | 1 | 0 | 0 |
| Medium | 1 | 9 | 26 | 64 | 0 | 0 | 0 |
| Large | 0 | 9 | 29 | 62 | 0 | 0 | 0 |
| d. Volunteers |  |  |  |  |  |  |  |
| Total | 2 | 23 | 29 | 36 | 8 | * | 1 |
| Small | 0 | 18 | 36 | 39 | 7 | 0 | 1 |
| Medium | 3 | 30 | 24 | 32 | 10 | 0 | 1 |
| Large | 3 | 19 | 28 | 40 | 9 | 2 | 0 |

Q28.  In the past five years, has your organization as a whole experienced
rapid growth, moderate growth, moderate decline, rapid decline, or has your
organization been stable, experiencing neither growth nor decline in the past
five years?

| All | Small | Medium | Large |  |
|---|---|---|---|---|
| 50 | 53 | 52 | 43 | Rapid growth |
| 41 | 39 | 41 | 43 | Moderate growth |
| 2 | 2 | 1 | 2 | Moderate decline |
| * | 1 | 0 | 0 | Rapid decline |
| 6 | 4 | 6 | 10 | Stable experiencing neither growth nor decline |
| * | 0 | 0 | 2 | Don't know |
| 0 | 0 | 0 | 0 | Refused |

Q29.   Which best describes your organization's leadership style.

| All | Small | Medium | Large | |
|---|---|---|---|---|
| 50 | 46 | 52 | 50 | We encourage discussion of issues, but the final decisions are made by the executive director or board |
| 43 | 43 | 43 | 43 | We discuss issues until we arrive at a consensus among the staff about how to deal with the issue |
| 6 | 11 | 3 | 5 | Don't know |
| 1 | 0 | 2 | 2 | Refused |

Q30.   How well does your organization's board understand (Insert)—very well, somewhat well, not too well, or not well at all?

| | Very well | Somewhat well | Not too well | Not well at all | Don't know | Refused |
|---|---|---|---|---|---|---|
| a. Its general responsibilities and duties as a board | | | | | | |
| Total | 62 | 37 | 1 | 0 | * | 0 |
| Small | 52 | 46 | 1 | 0 | 1 | 0 |
| Medium | 62 | 36 | 2 | 0 | 0 | 0 |
| Large | 74 | 26 | 0 | 0 | 0 | 0 |
| b. Its role in setting policy for your organization | | | | | | |
| Total | 72 | 26 | 2 | * | * | 0 |
| Small | 63 | 33 | 2 | 0 — | 1 | 0 |
| Medium | 79 | 20 | 1 | 0 | 0 | 0 |
| Large | 72 | 24 | 2 | 2 | 0 | 0 |
| c. Its role in overseeing your organization's performance | | | | | | |
| Total | 61 | 35 | 4 | 0 | * | 0 |
| Small | 50 | 43 | 6 | 0 | 1 | 0 |
| Medium | 63 | 34 | 3 | 0 | 0 | 0 |
| Large | 72 | 26 | 2 | 0 | 0 | 0 |

Q31.   To what extent do the staff and management in your organization feel comfortable taking risks and trying new things—a large extent, a fair extent, not too much, or not at all?

| All | Small | Medium | Large | |
|---|---|---|---|---|
| 59 | 58 | 63 | 55 | A large extent |
| 38 | 39 | 35 | 40 | A fair extent |
| 3 | 3 | 2 | 5 | Not too much |
| 0 | 0 | 0 | 0 | Not at all |
| 0 | 0 | 0 | 0 | Don't know |
| 0 | 0 | 0 | 0 | Refused |

Q32.   Which best describes communication among staff and management?

| All | Small | Medium | Large | |
|-----|-------|--------|-------|---|
| 4 | 2 | 4 | 9 | For the most part, staff and management communication is formal and businesslike, or |
| 92 | 93 | 94 | 86 | For the most part, staff and management communication is open and free-flowing |
| 3 | 3 | 2 | 3 | Don't know |
| 1 | 1 | 0 | 2 | Refused |

Q33.   Thinking about your organization's *internal management systems,* how much does your organization (Insert)—a great deal, a fair amount, not too much, or not at all?

| | A great deal | A fair amount | Not too much | Not at all | Don't know | Refused |
|---|------|------|------|------|------|------|
| a. Link staff pay to performance | | | | | | |
| Total | 24 | 42 | 23 | 9 | 1 | 0 |
| Small | 17 | 49 | 23 | 9 | 2 | 0 |
| Medium | 26 | 43 | 21 | 9 | 1 | 0 |
| Large | 34 | 29 | 28 | 9 | 0 | 0 |
| b. Use data to make decisions | | | | | | |
| Total | 43 | 48 | 9 | * | 0 | 0 |
| Small | 46 | 41 | 13 | 0 | 0 | 0 |
| Medium | 38 | 54 | 7 | 1 | 0 | 0 |
| Large | 50 | 45 | 5 | 0 | 0 | 0 |

Q34.   Does your organization have position descriptions for all its staff, most, some, a few, or none of your staff?

| All | Small | Medium | Large | |
|-----|-------|--------|-------|---|
| 86 | 82 | 85 | 93 | All |
| 11 | 11 | 14 | 7 | Most |
| 1 | 2 | 1 | 0 | Some |
| 0 | 0 | 0 | 0 | A few |
| 1 | 3 | 0 | 0 | None |
| * | 1 | 0 | 0 | Don't know |
| 0 | 0 | 0 | 0 | Refused |

Q35.  How many resources and programs does your organization provide for staff training—a lot, some, a few, or none?

| All | Small | Medium | Large | |
|---|---|---|---|---|
| 46 | 38 | 45 | 59 | A lot of programs or resources |
| 42 | 43 | 44 | 34 | Some |
| 9 | 11 | 9 | 7 | A few |
| 3 | 7 | 2 | 0 | None |
| * | 1 | 0 | 0 | Don't know |
| 0 | 0 | 0 | 0 | Refused |

Q36.  How many times a year, on average, does your board hold meetings?

| All | Small | Medium | Large | |
|---|---|---|---|---|
| 11 | 11 | 8 | 17 | Less than 4 times a year |
| 54 | 48 | 57 | 57 | 4–8 times a year |
| 35 | 41 | 35 | 26 | 9 or more times a year |
| 0 | 0 | 0 | 0 | Don't know |
| 0 | 0 | 0 | 0 | Refused |

Q37.  Is your organization's information technology very adequate, somewhat adequate, not too adequate, or not adequate at all?

| All | Small | Medium | Large | |
|---|---|---|---|---|
| 46 | 40 | 50 | 48 | Very adequate |
| 46 | 48 | 47 | 45 | Somewhat adequate |
| 6 | 10 | 3 | 5 | Not too adequate |
| 1 | 1 | 0 | 2 | Not adequate at all |
| * | 1 | 0 | 0 | Don't know |
| 0 | 0 | 0 | 0 | Refused |

Q37a.  Does your organization's accounting system make it very easy, somewhat easy, not too easy, or not at all easy to get an accurate accounting of your expenses and revenues whenever you need it?

| All | Small | Medium | Large | |
|---|---|---|---|---|
| 73 | 71 | 77 | 67 | Very easy |
| 22 | 26 | 17 | 28 | Somewhat easy |
| 4 | 3 | 5 | 5 | Not too easy |
| * | 0 | 1 | 0 | Not at all easy |
| 0 | 0 | 0 | 0 | Don't know |
| 0 | 0 | 0 | 0 | Refused |

Q38. Does your organization have a strategic plan for the future?

| All | Small | Medium | Large | |
|---|---|---|---|---|
| 91 | 86 | 95 | 93 | Yes |
| 8 | 13 | 5 | 7 | No |
| * | 1 | 0 | 0 | Don't know |
| 0 | 0 | 0 | 0 | Refused |

Q39. When was the planning process completed—in the last year,
1 to 2 years ago, 3 to 5 years ago or longer?

| All | Small | Medium | Large | |
|---|---|---|---|---|
| 44 | 44 | 42 | 48 | In last year |
| 22 | 22 | 22 | 20 | 1 to 2 years ago |
| 12 | 10 | 15 | 7 | 3 to 5 years ago |
| 0 | 0 | 0 | 0 | Longer |
| 22 | 22 | 21 | 24 | Currently in process (Volunteered) |
| * | 1 | 0 | 0 | Don't know |
| 0 | 0 | 0 | 0 | Refused |
| $n$ = 228 | $n$ = 77 | $n$ = 95 | $n$ = 54 | Based on those who say their organization has a strategic plan for the future |

Q40. The next set of questions is about nonprofit organizations in general. In your opinion, if a below-average-performing organization is trying to improve its performance, how important is it to improve its (Insert)—very important, somewhat important, not too important, or not important at all?

| | Very important | Somewhat important | Not too important | Not important at all | Don't know | Refused |
|---|---|---|---|---|---|---|
| a. External relationships—for example, the extent to which it collaborates with other organizations, has a diversified funding base, and measures its outcomes | | | | | | |
| Total | 64 | 33 | * | * | 1 | * |
| Small | 62 | 34 | 1 | 0 | 2 | 0 |
| Medium | 72 | 27 | 0 | 0 | 1 | 0 |
| Large | 55 | 41 | 0 | 2 | 0 | 2 |
| b. Internal organizational structure—for example, how decisions are made, how staff work together, and having a rainy day or reserve fund | | | | | | |
| Total | 68 | 30 | 1 | 0 | 1 | * |
| Small | 64 | 31 | 2 | 0 | 2 | 0 |
| Medium | 80 | 19 | 0 | 0 | 0 | 1 |
| Large | 53 | 47 | 0 | 0 | 0 | 0 |

(continued)

Q40.   The next set of questions is about nonprofit organizations in general. In your opinion, if a below-average performing organization is trying to improve its performance, how important is it to improve its (Insert)—very important, somewhat important, not too important, or not important at all? *(Continued)*

| | Very important | Somewhat important | Not too important | Not important at all | Don't know | Refused |
|---|---|---|---|---|---|---|
| c. Leadership—that is, how well the board understands its role, how well the leader motivates people and can fundraise | | | | | | |
| Total | 92 | 7 | 0 | 0 | * | * |
| Small | 90 | 9 | 0 | 0 | 1 | 0 |
| Medium | 94 | 6 | 0 | 0 | 0 | 0 |
| Large | 93 | 5 | 0 | 0 | 0 | 2 |
| d. Internal management systems—that is, the extent to which the organization has position descriptions, a strategic plan, and an accurate and fast accounting system | | | | | | |
| Total | 82 | 17 | 0 | 0 | 1 | 0 |
| Small | 74 | 24 | 0 | 0 | 1 | 0 |
| Medium | 85 | 14 | 0 | 0 | 1 | 0 |
| Large | 88 | 12 | 0 | 0 | 0 | 0 |

Q41.   And which of these four aspects of an organization—external relationships, internal organizational structure, leadership, and internal management systems—is the most important one for a below-average-performing organization to improve first?

| All | Small | Medium | Large | |
|---|---|---|---|---|
| 3 | 7 | 0 | 3 | External relationships |
| 12 | 22 | 9 | 2 | Internal organizational structure |
| 71 | 53 | 80 | 83 | Leadership |
| 12 | 16 | 9 | 12 | Internal management systems |
| 2 | 2 | 2 | 0 | Don't know |
| 0 | 0 | 0 | 0 | Refused |

Q42.  Which of the following components of an organization's external relationships is most important to improve first? Is it most important to . . .

| All | Small | Medium | Large | |
|---|---|---|---|---|
| 38 | 50 | 0 | 0 | Collaborate with other organizations |
| 13 | 0 | 0 | 50 | Have a diversified funding base |
| 0 | 0 | 0 | 0 | Rely on volunteers to deliver at least some services |
| 25 | 17 | 0 | 50 | Regularly survey clients regarding programs and services |
| 25 | 33 | 0 | 0 | Measure the results or outcomes of what they do |
| 0 | 0 | 0 | 0 | Generate at least some unrestricted revenue |
| 0 | 0 | 0 | 0 | Other (Volunteered) |
| 0 | 0 | 0 | 0 | None (Volunteered) |
| 0 | 0 | 0 | 0 | Don't know |
| 0 | 0 | 0 | 0 | Refused |
| $n = 8$ | $n = 6$ | $n = 0$ | $n = 2$ | Based on those who say that external relationships should be improved first |

Q43.  Which of the following components of an organization's internal organizational structure is most important to improve first? Is it most important to . . .

| All | Small | Medium | Large | |
|---|---|---|---|---|
| 13 | 20 | 0 | 0 | Have few layers of management between the top and bottom of the organization |
| 0 | 0 | 0 | 0 | Have demographically diverse staffs |
| 27 | 20 | 44 | 0 | Give staff authority to make routine decisions on their own |
| 30 | 30 | 33 | 0 | Have few barriers between organizational units |
| 0 | 0 | 0 | 0 | Have a "rainy day" or reserve fund |
| 27 | 25 | 22 | 100 | Encourage staff to work in teams |
| 0 | 0 | 0 | 0 | Use information technology to enhance performance |
| 0 | 0 | 0 | 0 | Other (Volunteered) |
| 3 | 5 | 0 | 0 | None (Volunteered) |
| 0 | 0 | 0 | 0 | Don't know |
| 0 | 0 | 0 | 0 | Refused |
| $n = 30$ | $n = 20$ | $n = 9$ | $n = 1$ | Based on those who say that internal organizational structure should be improved first |

Q44.   Which of the following components of an organization's leadership is most important to improve first? Is it most important for leaders to . . .

| All | Small | Medium | Large | |
|---|---|---|---|---|
| 11 | 8 | 14 | 10 | Have a participatory style of management |
| 1 | 0 | 0 | 4 | Fundraise |
| 24 | 21 | 28 | 23 | Have a clear understanding with their boards about their respective roles |
| 1 | 0 | 1 | 2 | Be charismatic |
| 29 | 33 | 30 | 21 | Know how to motivate people |
| 5 | 6 | 1 | 10 | Encourage risk taking |
| 0 | 0 | 0 | 0 | Foster open communication |
| 19 | 21 | 18 | 21 | Other (Volunteered) |
| 6 | 4 | 8 | 6 | None (Volunteered) |
| 1 | 0 | 1 | 0 | Don't know |
| 2 | 6 | 0 | 2 | Refused |
| $n = 177$ | $n = 48$ | $n = 80$ | $n = 48$ | Based on those who say that leadership should be improved first |

Q45.   Which of the following components of an organization's internal management systems is most important to improve first? Is it most important to . . .

| All | Small | Medium | Large | |
|---|---|---|---|---|
| 3 | 0 | 11 | 0 | Link staff pay to performance |
| 6 | 14 | 0 | 0 | Have position descriptions for staff |
| 3 | 0 | 11 | 0 | Have an accurate, fast accounting system |
| 3 | 0 | 0 | 14 | Have programs or resources for staff training |
| 6 | 14 | 0 | 0 | Hold regular board meetings (at least 4 times a year) |
| 0 | 0 | 0 | 0 | Have adequate information technology |
| 0 | 0 | 0 | 0 | Have a strategic plan for the future |
| 0 | 0 | 0 | 0 | Use data to make informed decisions |
| 42 | 50 | 33 | 29 | Other (Volunteered) |
| 19 | 21 | 11 | 29 | None (Volunteered) |
| 16 | 0 | 33 | 29 | Don't know |
| 0 | 0 | 0 | 0 | Refused |
| $n = 31$ | $n = 14$ | $n = 9$ | $n = 7$ | Based on those who say that internal management systems should be improved first |

Q46.  A variety of organizations are trying to improve nonprofit performance. How much has/have (Insert) contributed to improving *your* organization's performance—a great deal, a fair amount, not too much, or nothing at all?

| | A great deal | A fair amount | Not too much | Nothing at all | Don't know | Refused |
|---|---|---|---|---|---|---|
| **a. foundations** | | | | | | |
| Total | 27 | 39 | 22 | 13 | 0 | 0 |
| Small | 32 | 39 | 20 | 9 | 0 | 0 |
| Medium | 27 | 38 | 21 | 14 | 0 | 0 |
| Large | 19 | 38 | 26 | 17 | 0 | 0 |
| **b. the government** | | | | | | |
| Total | 8 | 21 | 26 | 45 | * | 0 |
| Small | 10 | 20 | 23 | 47 | 0 | 0 |
| Medium | 3 | 19 | 27 | 50 | 1 | 0 |
| Large | 12 | 26 | 28 | 34 | 0 | 0 |
| **c. graduate schools that train nonprofit executives and staff** | | | | | | |
| Total | 4 | 20 | 33 | 41 | 1 | 0 |
| Small | 3 | 11 | 26 | 59 | 1 | 0 |
| Medium | 6 | 22 | 37 | 33 | 2 | 0 |
| Large | 3 | 31 | 38 | 28 | 0 | 0 |
| **d. management service organizations** | | | | | | |
| Total | 8 | 25 | 34 | 30 | 4 | 0 |
| Small | 6 | 21 | 40 | 32 | 1 | 0 |
| Medium | 10 | 27 | 24 | 32 | 7 | 0 |
| Large | 7 | 28 | 40 | 24 | 2 | 0 |
| **e. external rating organizations** | | | | | | |
| Total | 8 | 18 | 24 | 46 | 4 | 0 |
| Small | 8 | 17 | 21 | 52 | 2 | 0 |
| Medium | 5 | 16 | 28 | 44 | 7 | 0 |
| Large | 12 | 22 | 24 | 41 | 0 | 0 |
| **f. providers of technical assistance** | | | | | | |
| Total | 15 | 47 | 28 | 10 | * | 0 |
| Small | 16 | 46 | 26 | 13 | 0 | 0 |
| Medium | 19 | 46 | 28 | 7 | 0 | 0 |
| Large | 9 | 48 | 33 | 9 | 2 | 0 |
| **g. associations of nonprofits** | | | | | | |
| Total | 14 | 44 | 27 | 15 | 0 | 0 |
| Small | 19 | 46 | 21 | 14 | 0 | 0 |
| Medium | 14 | 43 | 31 | 12 | 0 | 0 |
| Large | 7 | 40 | 31 | 22 | 0 | 0 |

Q47.   There have been a number of proposals over the past few years to improve nonprofit performance. Has/Have (Insert) improved *your* organization's performance a great deal, a fair amount, not too much, or not at all?

| | A great deal | A fair amount | Not too much | Nothing at all | Don't know | Refused |
|---|---|---|---|---|---|---|
| a. The creation of management standards | | | | | | |
| Total | 20 | 34 | 22 | 20 | 4 | 0 |
| Small | 13 | 32 | 27 | 23 | 4 | 0 |
| Medium | 18 | 35 | 20 | 23 | 4 | 0 |
| Large | 33 | 34 | 21 | 10 | 2 | 0 |
| b. The encouragement to collaborate with other nonprofits | | | | | | |
| Total | 37 | 36 | 20 | 8 | 0 | 0 |
| Small | 41 | 34 | 17 | 8 | 0 | 0 |
| Medium | 39 | 36 | 17 | 8 | 0 | 0 |
| Large | 28 | 38 | 28 | 7 | 0 | 0 |
| c. Making nonprofits more open to the public and media | | | | | | |
| Total | 19 | 35 | 22 | 22 | 2 | 0 |
| Small | 18 | 36 | 20 | 24 | 2 | 0 |
| Medium | 21 | 34 | 21 | 23 | 1 | 0 |
| Large | 19 | 36 | 28 | 16 | 2 | 0 |
| d. Reducing duplication and overlap among nonprofits through mergers and alliances | | | | | | |
| Total | 16 | 20 | 18 | 43 | 2 | 0 |
| Small | 16 | 16 | 22 | 44 | 2 | 0 |
| Medium | 17 | 24 | 14 | 44 | 1 | 0 |
| Large | 17 | 22 | 17 | 40 | 3 | 0 |
| e. Strengthening external reviews by the Better Business Bureau, GuideStar, and the National Charities Information Bureau | | | | | | |
| Total | 2 | 8 | 20 | 67 | 3 | 0 |
| Small | 0 | 6 | 21 | 70 | 3 | 0 |
| Medium | 3 | 9 | 15 | 69 | 4 | 0 |
| Large | 3 | 9 | 28 | 59 | 2 | 0 |
| f. The encouragement to do more strategic planning | | | | | | |
| Total | 51 | 33 | 8 | 7 | * | 0 |
| Small | 51 | 34 | 6 | 8 | 1 | 0 |
| Medium | 48 | 33 | 12 | 7 | 0 | 0 |
| Large | 57 | 29 | 7 | 7 | 0 | 0 |
| g. Giving executive directors greater access to training in running organizations | | | | | | |
| Total | 31 | 38 | 15 | 13 | 3 | 0 |
| Small | 29 | 40 | 14 | 13 | 3 | 0 |
| Medium | 34 | 35 | 14 | 14 | 3 | 0 |
| Large | 31 | 38 | 17 | 12 | 2 | 0 |

*(continued)*

Q47. There have been a number of proposals over the past few years to improve nonprofit performance. Has/Have (Insert) improved *your* organization's performance a great deal, a fair amount, not too much, or not at all? *(Continued)*

| | A great deal | A fair amount | Not too much | Nothing at all | Don't know | Refused |
|---|---|---|---|---|---|---|
| h. Encouraging executive directors to stay in their jobs for longer periods | | | | | | |
| Total | 37 | 24 | 10 | 24 | 6 | 0 |
| Small | 34 | 21 | 13 | 27 | 4 | 0 |
| Medium | 39 | 26 | 6 | 21 | 8 | 0 |
| Large | 36 | 26 | 10 | 24 | 3 | 0 |
| i. Encouraging foundations to provide more funding for capacity building | | | | | | |
| Total | 38 | 27 | 16 | 16 | 2 | 0 |
| Small | 37 | 30 | 16 | 16 | 2 | 0 |
| Medium | 40 | 24 | 16 | 18 | 2 | 0 |
| Large | 36 | 26 | 19 | 16 | 3 | 0 |
| j. An increased emphasis on outcomes measurement | | | | | | |
| Total | 37 | 42 | 12 | 8 | 1 | 0 |
| Small | 28 | 47 | 13 | 11 | 1 | 0 |
| Medium | 40 | 36 | 17 | 6 | 1 | 0 |
| Large | 47 | 45 | 3 | 5 | 0 | 0 |
| k. Management assistance grants | | | | | | |
| Total | 12 | 20 | 15 | 49 | 5 | 0 |
| Small | 16 | 27 | 10 | 44 | 3 | 0 |
| Medium | 11 | 15 | 13 | 56 | 5 | 0 |
| Large | 7 | 17 | 24 | 45 | 7 | 0 |
| l. Increased openness to using standard business tools or techniques | | | | | | |
| Total | 42 | 40 | 11 | 6 | 1 | 0 |
| Small | 38 | 37 | 14 | 10 | 1 | 0 |
| Medium | 43 | 43 | 10 | 3 | 1 | 0 |
| Large | 43 | 41 | 7 | 7 | 2 | 0 |
| m. More active donor involvement or oversight | | | | | | |
| Total | 24 | 34 | 18 | 24 | 1 | 0 |
| Small | 24 | 34 | 13 | 27 | 1 | 0 |
| Medium | 22 | 34 | 21 | 23 | 0 | 0 |
| Large | 24 | 31 | 19 | 22 | 3 | 0 |

D1.  Sex

| All | Small | Medium | Large | |
|---|---|---|---|---|
| 45 | 39 | 42 | 62 | Male |
| 55 | 61 | 58 | 38 | Female |

D2.  What is your age?

| All | Small | Medium | Large | |
|---|---|---|---|---|
| 2 | 3 | 0 | 2 | 18–29 |
| 13 | 24 | 8 | 5 | 30–39 |
| 28 | 26 | 32 | 22 | 40–49 |
| 48 | 39 | 52 | 55 | 50–59 |
| 10 | 8 | 8 | 16 | 60–69 |
| 0 | 0 | 0 | 0 | 70 or older |
| 0 | 0 | 0 | 0 | Don't know |
| 0 | 0 | 0 | 0 | Refused |

D3.  Do you have a graduate degree or advanced training in management?

| All | Small | Medium | Large | |
|---|---|---|---|---|
| 43 | 41 | 45 | 43 | Graduate degree |
| 19 | 26 | 13 | 19 | Advanced training |
| 14 | 8 | 18 | 17 | Both (Volunteered) |
| 24 | 26 | 24 | 19 | Neither (Volunteered) |
| * | 0 | 0 | 2 | Don't know |
| 0 | 0 | 0 | 0 | Refused |

D4.  Which of these best describes your race and ethnicity? White, black or African American, Hispanic or Latino, Asian, or something else?

| All | Small | Medium | Large | |
|---|---|---|---|---|
| 87 | 84 | 90 | 84 | White |
| 7 | 7 | 5 | 10 | Black or African-American |
| 4 | 7 | 1 | 3 | Hispanic or Latino |
| 1 | 0 | 3 | 0 | Asian |
| 1 | 2 | 0 | 2 | Other |
| 0 | 0 | 0 | 0 | Don't know |
| * | 0 | 1 | 0 | Refused |

# Notes

## Chapter One

1. See Independent Sector, *The New Nonprofit Almanac in Brief* (Washington: 2001).

2. "Gifts to Rescuers Divide Survivors," *New York Times*, December 2, 2001, p. A1.

3. David Haldane, "Charity Donations Down, Demands Up," *Los Angeles Times*, December 17, 2001, p. A1.

4. Penelope Wang, "Wise Giving Guide," *Money,* December 2001, p. 176.

5. National Public Radio, *Morning Edition,* January 3, 2002.

6. Quoted in Michelle Kessler, "Tech Stock Drop Hits Charities' Bottom Line," *USA Today,* January 3, 2002, p. 3B.

7. "Trimming Holiday Hopes," *Chronicle of Philanthropy*, December 13, 2001, found at http://philanthropy.com/free/articles/v14/i05/05000601.htm.

8. Center on Philanthropy, *Philanthropic Giving Index, December, 2001* (Indiana University, 2001).

9. See American Association of Fundraising Counsel, news release on the Center on Philanthropy study, September 27, 2001.

10. Center on Philanthropy, *Philanthropic Giving Index*, p. 7.

11. Kathleen Teltsch, "Charitable Giving Rose to $124 Billion in 1992," *New York Times,* May 26, 1993, p. A17.

12. Paul C. Light and Judith M. Labiner, "A Vote of Renewed Confidence: How Americans View Presidential Appointees in the Wake of the September 11 Terrorist Attacks," Presidential Appointee Initiative report, October 2001. The first survey was conducted between June 18 and July 18, 2001, and the second from September 27 to October 6. Total sample size was 1,003 in the first survey and 1,033 in the second, which yields a margin of error of approximately plus or minus three percentage points. The survey was conducted on behalf of the center

by Princeton Survey Research Associates (PSRA), under the direction of Mary McIntosh, vice president of PSRA.

13. See National Science Foundation, "Public Bounces Back after September 11 Attacks, National Study Shows," press release, October 24, 2001.

14. Richard Morin and Claudia Dean, "The Ideas Industry," *Washington Post*, January 15, 2002, p. A17.

15. Independent Sector, *Giving and Volunteering in the United States* (Washington: 1999).

16. Gary Langer, "Water's Edge: Greater Trust in Government Limited to National Security," ABCnews.com, January 16, 2002.

17. Deborah Sontag, "Who Brought Bernadine Healy Down," *New York Times Magazine*, December 23, 2001, p. 38.

18. Fox News Network, *The O'Reilly Factor,* transcript, October 5, 2001.

19. "O'Reilly Rips Celeb Phonies," *New York Post*, November 2, 2001, p. 10.

20. Diana B. Henriques and David Barstow, "Red Cross Pledges Entire Terror Fund to Sept. 11 Victims," *New York Times*, November 13, p. A1.

21. Bill O'Reilly, "A Sign from the Red Cross," *Washington Times*, November 19, 2001, p. A15.

22. David Barstow, "In Congress, Harsh Words for Red Cross," *New York Times*, November 6, 2001, p. B1.

23. Fox News Network, *The O'Reilly Factor,* transcript, November 26, 2001.

24. Lena H. Sun and Jacqueline L. Salmon, "Sept. 11 Funds Wrestle with What's Fair," *Washington Post*, December 10, 2001, p. A14.

25. See Diana B. Henriques, "Holding the Victims' Purse Strings, Uneasily," *New York Times*, December 11, 2001, p. B1.

26. "Wise Giving Guide," *Money*, December 2001, p. 176.

27. "Flashpoint Research Report: Bay Area Nonprofits Respond to Economic Downturn," *CompassPoint*, November 2001.

28. The survey on the Red Cross and United Way news interest was conducted on behalf of the Center for Public Service by Princeton Survey Research Associates from December 10 to 16, 2001, and involved 1,011 respondents, yielding a margin of error of plus or minus 5 percent. For the rest of the news interest items, see Pew Research Center for the People & the Press, *Terrorism Transforms News Interest* (Washington: December 19, 2001).

29. These general confidence questions were asked of just half the December sample, yielding a sample size of 492.

30. The size of this sample was 519.

# Chapter 2

1. Paul C. Light, "To Restore and Renew," *Government Executive*, November 1, 2001.

2. Herbert Kaufman, *Are Governmental Organizations Immortal?* (Brookings, 1976).

3. For a discussion of these welfare-to-work competitions, see Mary Bryna Sanger, "When the Private Sector Competes," Brookings *Reform Watch*, no. 3, October 2001.

4. Edward Skloot, "Evolution or Extinction: A Strategy for Nonprofits in the Marketplace," *Nonprofit and Voluntary Sector Quarterly*, vol. 29, no. 2 (2000), pp. 315–24.

5. Paul C. Light, *The New Public Service* (Brookings, 1999).

6. Data available from the Foundation Center's interactive database, at http://fdncenter.org/fc_stats/index.html. My thanks to Elizabeth Hubbard for her help collecting this information.

7. Paul C. Light, *Making Nonprofits Work: A Report on the Tides of Non-profit Management Reform* (Brookings, 2000).

8. See Pierre Mourier and Martin Smith, *Conquering Organization Change: How to Succeed Where Most Companies Fail* (New York: CEP Press, 2001).

9. Melissa M. Stone, Barbara Bigelow, and William Crittenden, "Research on Strategic Management in Nonprofit Organizations," *Administration & Society*, vol. 31, no. 3 (1999), pp. 378–423.

10. See Cassandra Benjamin, *Broken Yardstick: Administrative Cost Rates as a Measure of Nonprofit Effectiveness* (San Francisco: CompassPoint, 2000).

11. Daniel P. Forbes, "Measuring the Unmeasurable: Empirical Studies of Nonprofit Organizational Effectiveness from 1977 to 1997," *Nonprofit and Voluntary Sector Quarterly*, vol. 27, no. 2 (1998), p. 183.

12. Barbara Blumenthal, "How Can We Help? A Comparison of Capacity Building Programs," unpublished manuscript, April 25, 2001, p. 2.

13. Robert D. Herman and David O. Renz, "Theses on Nonprofit Organizational Effectiveness," *Nonprofit and Voluntary Sector Quarterly*, vol. 28, no. 2 (1999), pp. 107–26.

14. The list of active award programs includes Nashville's First Foundation Awards of Achievement in Nonprofit Management, which focus on team building, making a difference, and innovation in action; the Marvin Runyon Leadership Award, which recognizes nonprofits that excel in turnaround management; the Ericson Internet Community Award (ERICA), which rewards nonprofit groups that use the Internet to improve their services and strengthen their communities; the Peter F. Drucker Award for Nonprofit Innovation, which is given to a nonprofit organization whose performance exemplifies Drucker's definition of innovation as change that creates a new dimension of performance; the Excellence in Nonprofit Leadership Award, which carries a $25,000 cash prize to honor an outstanding Silicon Valley nonprofit leader; the John Gardner Leadership Award, which recognizes individuals working in the voluntary sector who build, mobilize, or unify people, institutions, or causes; and the Leadership IS Award, established to honor outstanding organizations for investing in the people of the independent sector.

15. An additional Internet survey of forty-five capacity builders assembled for a spring 2001 conference by the Packard Foundation provided general confirmation of the trends found in the opinion leaders' survey, while an Internet survey of

seventy-two Philadelphia Fund grantees of the Pew Charitable Trusts provided some validation of the trends found in the executives' survey.

## Chapter 3

1. These interviews were conducted by Elizabeth Hubbard on behalf of the Center for Public Service.

2. For a discussion of this map of organizational life, see Paul C. Light, *Sustaining Innovation: Creating Nonprofit and Government Organizations That Innovate Naturally* (San Francisco: Jossey-Bass, 1995), chap. 1.

3. See Paul C. Light, *The New Public Service* (Brookings, 1999), chap. 4.

4. Robert Behn, *Leadership Counts: Lessons for Public Managers* (Harvard University Press, 1991), pp. 216–17.

5. Harold L. Angle and Andrew H. Van de Ven, "Suggestions for Managing the Innovation Journey," in Andrew H. Van de Ven, Harold L. Angle, and Marshall Scott Poole, eds., *Research on the Management of Innovation: The Minnesota Studies* (HarperCollins, 1989), p. 679.

6. Angle and Van de Ven, "Managing the Innovation Journey," p. 681.

## Chapter 4

1. This interview and the other long interviews with executives were conducted by Elizabeth Hubbard.

2. The following pages echo the characteristics found in high-performing private firms, at least as inventoried by James Collins, first in his book with Jerry I. Porras, *Built to Last: Successful Habits of Visionary Companies* (HarperBusiness, 1994), and by himself in *Good to Great* (HarperBusiness, 2001).

3. See Paul C. Light, "The State of the Nonprofit Public Service," *Nonprofit Quarterly*, forthcoming, September 2002.

4. For an introduction to board development, see Mark J. Light, *The Strategic Board: The Step by Step to High Impact Governance* (John Wiley, 2001).

## Chapter 5

1. For an introduction to nonprofit life-cycle theory, see Susan Stevens, *Nonprofit Lifecycles: Stage-Based Wisdom for Nonprofit Capacity*, forthcoming (2002).

2. These combinations leave thirty respondents, or 12 percent, behind, whether because they chose resilient or rigorous as the primary characteristic of a high-performing organization, or because they refused to answer one or the other question. Fourteen of the respondents who did pick resilient or rigorous favored the decisive leader, while sixteen favored the reflective leader.

# Index